# THE THREE STARS

## and other SELECTIONS

# THE THREE STARS and other SELECTIONS

## More Amazing Lists
### for Trivia Lovers

Jefferson **DAVIS** & Andrew **PODNIEKS**

ECW PRESS

CANADIAN CATALOGUING IN PUBLICATION DATA
Davis, Jefferson, 1962–
The three stars and other selections : more amazing lists for trivia lovers

ISBN 1-55022-427-1

1. National Hockey League — Miscellanea.  2. Hockey Miscellanea.
I. Podnieks, Andrew.  II. Title

GV847.D426 2000          796.962'64          C00-931709-0

Cover and text design by Tania Craan
Layout by Mary Bowness
Printed by Transcontinental


Distributed in Canada by General Distribution Services,
325 Humber Blvd., Etobicoke, Ontario M9W 7C3

Distributed in the United States by LPC Group,
1436 West Randolph Street, Chicago, Illinois, USA 60607

Published by ECW PRESS
2120 Queen Street East, Suite 200,
Toronto, Ontario, M4E 1E2
www.ecw.ca/press

The publication of *The Three Stars and Other Selections* has been generously supported by the Government of Canada through the Book Publishing Industry Development Program.

**Canadä**

PRINTED AND BOUND IN CANADA

# CONTENTS

# Ten **ODDITIES** About the Three
## **STAR SELECTION**

**1** The naming of the three best players in a game originated as a promotion for Three Star gasoline advertised during the Hot Stove League on radio broadcasts of Leaf games in the 1940s. As a result, the selections were a particularly Canadian tradition for many years.

**2** When Foster Hewitt made the selections, he invariably chose one or both goaltenders. Usually, however, the selections were made by one of the Hot Stovers – Wes McKnight, Baldy Cotton, Court Benson, Elmer Ferguson.

The Hot Stove League of Wes McKnight, Baldy Cotton, Court Benson, and Elmer Ferguson entertained fans across Canada via the Toronto Maple Leafs' radio broadcasts in the 1940s.

**3** The stars used to be announced 1–2–3, the most prominent receiving immediate acclaim. However, some U.S. based teams such as Buffalo reversed the order in the 1970s as the drama built from the third star to second to first.

**4** It wasn't until games were televised that the honoured players actually skated out onto the ice and their names announced over the p.a. system at Maple Leaf Gardens or the Montreal Forum.

**5** Molson breweries began sponsoring the selections in 1973 when it introduced the Molson Cup trophy for Canadian teams. This was presented to each of these clubs on a monthly and yearly basis of those players who were named the three stars most frequently.

**6** Mike Walton of the Leafs was named on of the Three Stars in eleven consecutive games.

**7** Rocket Richard was once named all Three Stars after scoring five goals in a playoff game against Toronto.

**8** Wayne Gretzky played his last two NHL games in Ottawa on April 15, 1999, and three nights later in Madison Square Garden. In both games, he was named the only Sta of the game.

**9** Eddie Shack was rarely named a Star, but when chosen he was by far the most exciting. He would skate madly out to centre ice and then do a quick twirl with his stick high in the air to acknowledge the cheers of the fans.

**10** One night in Toronto, Barclay Plager of the St. Louis Blues played a particularly inspired game but also enrage the Leafs' fans in the process. When coming back out as one of the Three Stars, he blew a kiss to his "admirers."

# Last **NUMBER ONE** Goalies
# of the **ORIGINAL SIX**

**1**

### TORONTO
Johnny Bower & Terry Sawchuk

The Leafs actually used five goalies during the 1966–67 regular season, Bower and Sawchuk as well as Bruce Gamble, Gary Smith, and Al Smith. But come the playoffs it was the two forty-year-olds who took the Leafs to the Stanley Cup. While both men were to play parts of the first few years of expansion, this was, for all intents and purposes, their swan song in the NHL.

**2**

### MONTREAL
Charlie Hodge / Rogie Vachon / Gump Worsley

Although Hodge played 37 games for the Habs, Vachon and Worsley played 19 and 18 games respectively. All three were at different stages: Vachon was just beginning what was to be a superb career in the league; Worsley, though well into his thirties, still had many years to go with Minnesota even though he had been in the league more than a decade; and Hodge was trying hard to become the heir to Jacques Plante's throne, but without much consistent success.

**3**

### CHICAGO
Denis Dejordy / Glenn Hall

This was a class old/young tandem. Hall had been sent to the Hawks in the deal that took Ted Lindsay out of Detroit for his attempts to form a players' union, and Hall's career had been long and glorious to this point. Dejordy was the youngster who was apprenticing under the Hall of Famer, hoping to inherit his mantle and skill. Dejordy, however, proved to be only a stop gap between Hall and the soon-to-be-great Hawks' goalies, Tony Esposito.

### 4    NEW YORK
Ed Giacomin

Giacomin played half the Rangers' games the previous season, and he was in goal for 68 of the team's 70 games in '66–'67 making him the busiest goalie in the league. He was to have a great career with the Rangers before being traded by Emile Francis in a stunning move to Detroit. Giacomin also led the NHL with nine shutouts this season.

### 5    DETROIT
Roger Crozier

An enigmatic puck-stopper, "Crow" burst onto the NHL scene during the 1966 playoffs for the Wings in the Stanley Cup finals against Montreal. He almost single-handedly kept the team in the series, and although they eventually lost in six games, he was awarded the Conn Smythe Trophy. This was his fourth year as the number one man for the Wings, and although his star burned bright in Motown, it didn't burn for very long. Health problems affected his play, and by the early seventies his time in the league had passed.

### 6    BOSTON
Eddie Johnston / Gerry Cheevers / Bernie Parent

As in Montreal, these three were at different stages of their careers. Parent was about to become a great goalie with Toronto, briefly, and then Philadelphia for two Stanley Cups, and in this his second year in the league he was still learning. Cheevers had started in Toronto, but it was in Boston that he was to spend the best and most successful part of his career, though he moved to the WHA in 1972 for many years. Johnston had been with the Bruins since 1962 and was a steady if unspectacular goaler for the Beantowners.

# Ten NHL **PLAYERS** to **BECOME** NHL **OFFICIALS**

**1**

### KING CLANCY

The grand-daddy of all players, Clancy's career as a zebra was almost as legendary as his life as a player. He blew his whistle for more than a decade, and was the most respected and popular of officials. He was the number one man in the league, and although players argued with him long and hard, his opinion was good as gold for most.

**2**

### JOE PRIMEAU

After a great career with the Maple Leafs, Primeau remained in the game for a few years as a linesman. His calling, however, was a coach, and he soon retired from the ice to boss the bench first of the St. Mike's Majors and then the Leafs.

**3**

### RED HORNER

One of the toughest defensemen of his era, he led the league in penalty minutes for eight straight years. After retiring in 1940, he was asked by NHL president Frank Calder to officiate games in his home of Toronto to give added respect to the officiating crew, but after three seasons he called it quits and went into private business.

**4**

### GAYE STEWART

Like Red Horner, Stewart applied for a job as a linesman when NHL president Clarence Campbell sought to maintain a player presence among his officiating staff. He also reffed in the American league, but like Horner soon retired to pursue business interests outside the game.

**5**

### MUSH MARCH

After 17 seasons with the Chicago Blackhawks, March began a career in the striped shirt shortly after the end of the war. He stayed in the game a number of years as a referee, and retired having avoided much of the controversy officials managed to attract for their efforts.

## 6 ART DUNCAN

Duncan played in the NHL for only five seasons with Detroit and Toronto, but his career as a referee was as brief during the 1930s as his 156-game career was unspectacular during the '20s.

## 7 BABE DYE

One of the finest pure goal-scorers of early hockey, Dye became a referee after he retired in 1931, staying closest to his home in Toronto for most of his career. He reffed at many levels in the city, not just the NHL, and became one of the most popular figures in Toronto for his contributions to the game locally.

## 8 BERT McCAFFERY

After winning a gold medal with the Toronto Granites at the 1924 Olympic Winter Games, McCaffery played seven years in the NHL with Toronto, Pittsburgh, and then Montreal where he won a Cup with the Canadiens in 1930. He, too, joined the whistle-blowing fraternity for a short time in the 1930s.

## 9 KEVIN MAGUIRE

The most recent player to become a ref, Maguire was a hard-working, fourth line forward who was counted on for a physical presence on his teams. But his career was far from brilliant, and he retired early so that he could concentrate on officiating. He spent a few seasons learning the job in the AHL, and for the last couple of years has seen his number of NHL assignments steadily increase.

## 10 PAUL STEWART

Stewart had 74 penalty minutes in 21 games with the Quebec Nordiques, his only year in the NHL. Like Maguire, he saw a career in hockey more rewarding as a referee and left the game at age 26 in 1980 to concentrate on these abilities. He is now one of the most senior and well-respected officials in the game.

# Seven **AMAZING** Facts about
# **HILDA RANSCOMBE**

**1** She was a founding members of the Preston Rivulettes, the women's hockey team that went virtually undefeated during their decade of play, from 1930 until the start of the war in 1939.

**2** She was the leading scorer with the team for ten years, a gifted playmaker and stickhandler both, who scored in almost every game she played. She was also noted for her back-checking during a time when that skill was practised by few.

**3** Her sister, Nellie, also played with the Rivs. She was the goalie for ten years, and never had a backup and was never pulled. A rough though diminutive player, she was as competitive in keeping the puck out of the net as Hilda was at putting it in at the other end.

**4** Hilda was a great ballplayer. In fact, the Rivs hockey team was composed mostly of baseball players from a team bearing the same nickname. Hilda was a pitcher, and Nellie a catcher, and the Rivs won as many provincial softball titles as they did hockey championships.

**5** Much like Wayne Gretzky as a child in Brantford, Ontario, Hilda practised her skating by herself on the Speed River in Preston, teaching herself the art of the game and working on her stick-handling and shooting.

**6** The Rivs often played and practised in the nearby Arena in Galt. One day, at a time they were scheduled to go on the ice, a boys' team was playing. They invited the Rivs to play, and Hilda skated through the entire team to score a goal.

**7**    Although Hilda was called the best woman player in Canada, she is not in the Hockey Hall of Fame. In fact, there are no women in the Hall, even though her reputation has only grown over the years to the point that she has been called the Wayne Gretzky of women's hockey.

During the 1930s Hilda Ranscombe of the Preston Rivulettes dominated women's hockey to the same extent that Wayne Gretzky did in the NHL.

# CURRENT NHL COACHES Who Once PLAYED IN THE NHL

**1**

### MARC CRAWFORD, VANCOUVER

A draft choice of the Canucks in 1980, Crawford went on to play parts of six years with the Canucks, never staying in the NHL for a full season. From 1981 to 1987 he split his time between the farm teams in Dallas and Fredericton and the Canucks. In 1985–86, he had 25 points in 54 games, but after two more seasons in the minors he retired to focus on coaching.

**2**

### KEVIN LOWE, EDMONTON

Lowe played 19 years in the NHL, most notably during the great Edmonton dynasty of the 1980s. He won five Stanley Cups with the Oilers and then another with the Rangers in 1994 before finishing his 1,254-game career with the Oilers again. He became the team's head coach in the summer of 1999.

**3**

### PAT QUINN, TORONTO

Like many a coach, Quinn once played for the team he currently coaches. He skated for the Leafs from 1968 to 1970 before being claimed by Vancouver in the Expansion Draft. Two years later, he was again exposed and claimed by Atlanta when it joined the league in 1972. Quinn stayed with the original Flames for five years before retiring.

**4**

### ALAIN VIGNEAULT, MONTREAL

Selected 167th overall by St. Louis in the 1981 draft, Vigneault played all of 42 games in the NHL, with the Blues during the years 1981–83. He scored two goals and seven points before retiring. After coaching eight seasons in the Quebec junior league, he became Montreal's head coach in 1997.

## 5 CRAIG HARTSBURG, ANAHEIM

Hartsburg's ten-year NHL career consisted of 570 games, all with the Minnesota North Stars. Selected 6th overall at the 1979 draft, he was a defenseman with a great reputation who went on to captain the team for six years until injuries forced him into retirement. He coached for Guelph in the OHL and was an assistant in Philadelphia and Minnesota before becoming Chicago's head coach for three seasons. He was named head coach for Anaheim in 1998.

## 6 CURT FRASER, ATLANTA

Fraser spent 12 seasons in the NHL with Vancouver, Chicago, and Minnesota. He scored 25 goals in a season five times and he was in the playoffs the first nine years of his career. Prior to being named head coach of the expansion Thrashers, Fraser coached for six years in the IHL, with Milwaukee and Orlando.

## 7 LINDY RUFF, BUFFALO

A tough, hard-working defenseman for 12 years in the NHL, Ruff has brought a similar character and determination to his coaching. He spent nearly ten years with the Sabres before finishing with the Rangers, and in 1985–86 he scored 20 goals for Buffalo. A former captain of the team, he replaced Ted Nolan as the Sabres' coach in the summer of 1997.

## 8 BUTCH GORING, NEW YORK ISLANDERS

A four-time Stanley Cup winner with these same Islander during the height of the franchise's success, Goring finds himself in a much tougher position with a team that has missed the playoffs the previous six seasons. Goring played 17 years in the league, also with Boston and Los Angeles, during a career that endured more than 1,100 games.

## 9 JOEL QUENNEVILLE, ST. LOUIS

A resourceful and underrated defensive defenseman for
ʒ years in the NHL, Quenneville dressed for 803 games from
)78 to 1991 with Toronto, Colorado, New Jersey, Hartford, and
'ashington. He played only 32 career playoff games and began
s future career as a player/coach for the St. John's Maple Leafs
1991–92.

## 10 DARRYL SUTTER, SAN JOSE

One of the great six Sutter brothers from Viking, Alberta, Darryl had the shortest career in the NHL of his brothers, reduced to just 406 games because of injury. He played his entire eight-year career with Chicago and is blessed with one of the finest young teams in the league.

## 11 STEVE LUDZIK, TAMPA BAY

An NHLer from 1981 to 1990, Ludzik controls the worst team in the league. As a skater, he was a part-timer most of his career with Chicago and Buffalo. He coached five years of minor pro before making the jump to the NHL, winning the IHL's Turner Cup championship in 1997.

## 12 RON WILSON, WASHINGTON

Drafted 133rd overall by Montreal in 1976, it wasn't until three years later that Wilson played his first NHL game with the Winnipeg Jets. He spent nine years in the Jets' organization before being traded to St. Louis, and his career ended as it had begun, in Montreal. On August 20, 1993 he signed with the Canadiens as a free agent and played his final 48 games in the NHL with the Habs.

## 13 LARRY ROBINSON, NEW JERSEY DEVILS

A Hall of Famer as a player, Robinson is one of only a few players to win the Cup as both skater and bench boss. In fact, he won six Cups with Montreal, including four in a row in the late '70s, and he won the Cup just last year with New Jersey after taking over as head coach late in the season when Robbie Ftorek was fired.

## 14 JACQUES LEMAIRE, MINNESOTA WILD

One of the better two-way centres during his prime, Lemaire was a teammate of Robinson during the team's glory years. He went on to coach the Devils to the team's first Cup during the lockout-shortened '94-'95 season, but his stifling trap defence is likely to make fans in Minnesota anything but wild.

## 15 RON LOW, NEW YORK RANGERS

By coaching just one game with the Rangers, Low made history. He became the only former NHL goalie to coach two different NHL teams. In other words, previous goalies turned coaches were viewed as an experiment. When they were gone from the team, no other NHL team felt confidence enough in him to give the goaler-coach another chance.

## 16 CRAIG RAMSAY, PHILADELPHIA FLYERS

Ironically, Ramsay's best friend was Roger Neilson, the man he replaced under controversial circumstances in 1999–2000. As a player, Ramsay was a reliable defensive defenseman with some offensive talent who played all of his 14 seasons with Buffalo.

# First **TEN COACHES** of the
# Minnesota **NORTH STARS**

**1**

### WREN BLAIR

Blair led the expansion North Stars to 69 points and a fourth place finish in 1967–68. They defeated Los Angeles in the first round of the playoffs and came within one game of the Stanley Cup final before losing to St. Louis. Blair stepped down to focus on the duties of general manager after the team got off to a disappointing 12–20–9 start the next year. He returned briefly in 1969–70 to replace Charlie Burns.

**2**

### JOHN MUCKLER

Many fans would be surprised to find Muckler's name as the Minnesota head coach in the late 1960s. He replaced Wren Blair halfway through the 1968–69 season. Unfortunately, the struggling team played even worse under Muckler and had a dismal record of 6–23–6.

**3**

### CHARLIE BURNS

Burns started the 1969–70 season as the North Stars player-coach but was replaced by Wren Blair before the end of the schedule. The franchise struggled in its second and third seasons before its fortunes improved. Burns guided the team to a 10–22–12 record and later returned in 1974–75 for 42 games.

**4**

### JACKIE GORDON

Recognizable because of his trademark fedora, Gordon led the North Stars back to respectability before his career was ended by poor health. During his first year, the North Stars extended eventual Cup-winner Montreal to six games in the semi-finals. The following season, the Stars recorded 86 points but were upset by St. Louis in the first round of the post-season.

## 5

### PARKER MacDONALD

Former NHLer MacDonald replaced Jackie Gordon early in the 1973–74 season. The club was off to a poor start when he took over and matters did not improve. Under MacDonald the team went 20–30–11 and finished a dismal seventh in the West Division standings.

## 6

### TED HARRIS

A former North Stars defenseman and captain, Harris took over as a coach after he retired as a player in 1975. The team was competitive on most nights but did not win as many games as hoped. Harris' record as the Minnesota bench boss was an unflattering 48–104–27.

## 7

### ANDRÉ BEAULIEU

Beaulieu tried his hand at reversing the North Stars' fortunes in 1977–78 but did not fare any better than most of his predecessors. He was let go after the team got off to a slothful 6–23–3 start.

## 8

### LOU NANNE

A popular forward when he played for Minnesota, Nanne was the team's general manager when he took over as coach on an interim basis in 1977–78 after firing Beaulieu. The team continued to struggle with a 7–18–4 mark but was strengthened in the off-season when it was merged with the former Cleveland Barons franchise.

## 9

### HARRY HOWELL

One of the top defensemen of his era, Howell had a short eleven-game sample of life as an NHL coach in 1978–79. When the team stumbled out of the gate with a 3–6–2 record, he was replaced by Glen Sonmor.

## 10 GLEN SONMOR

After taking over from Harry Howell, Sonmor became the franchise's most successful coach up to that point. The Stars still missed the playoffs but there was promise led by Calder trophy winner Bobby Smith. The next year, the team won 36 games and reached the semi-finals. In 1980–81, Sonmor guided the North Stars all the way to the Stanley Cup finals where they lost in five games to the New York Islanders.

Coach Glen Sonmor guided the Minnesota North Stars to the Stanley Cup final in 1981.

# Eleven **ODD FACTS** About the
## **500-GOAL CLUB**

**1**   Of the 27 players to have scored 500 career goals, Lanny McDonald is the only one to have exactly 500.

**2**   Mike Bossy, Wayne Gretzky, and Jari Kurri are the only players to score #500 into an empty net.

**3**   Gretzky and Mark Messier are the only ones to get the goal in November. The most popular month has been March when six of the 27 players have scored their 500th.

**4**   Joe Mullen and Dave Andreychuk scored their historic goals on consecutive nights, March 14 and 15, 1997.

**5**   Toronto is the only Original Six team not to have had a player score his 500th while with the team. Four times a player has scored his 500th while with the Montreal Canadiens.

**6**   The last Hall of Fame goalie to give up a 500th goal was Ed Giacomin on Bobby Hull in 1970.

**7**   Patrick Roy is the only goalie to give up two 500th goals, to Steve Yzerman and Joe Mullen.

**8**   Jari Kurri, on October 17, 1992, was the first non-Canadian to score 500 goals in the NHL.

**9**   Joe Mullen is the only American player to score 500. He did so in his 1,052nd game while playing for Pittsburgh.

**10** It took Johnny Bucyk 1,370 games to get 500, longer than any other player. Wayne Gretzky was the fastest, scoring 500 in just 575 games.

**11** Pat Verbeek and Gordie Howe are the only two 500-goal men never to have had a 50-goal season.

# Most **GAMES MISSED** by an
# **ART ROSS TROPHY** Winner

## 24   MARIO LEMIEUX — 1992-93
(28.58%)

Incredibly, Lemieux missed more than a quarter of the season and still won the scoring title, in large part because Wayne Gretzky also missed much of the season with a bad back. Runner-up Pat Lafontaine finished a distant 12 points behind Lemieux, who had 160 points in just 60 games.

## 19   JAROMIR JAGR — 1999-2000
(23.17%)

Jagr's season was full of absences for brief periods totalling 19 games, but when he played he established himself as the league's best player, winning the Art Ross for the third consecutive year and fourth during his career. In second place was Pavel Bure who finished just two points behind Jagr. He missed eight games himself with injuries, otherwise he likely would have overtaken Jagr.

Pittsburgh Penguins' superstar Mario Lemieux bids adieu to the hometown fans for the last time during the 1997 Playoffs.

## 12 MARIO LEMIEUX — 1991-92
(20%)

This race was a little closer, but injuries again ate into Lemieux's season. Still, his 131 points were eight better than teammate Kevin Stevens's. Lemieux won the Art Ross playing just 64 games.

## 12 MARIO LEMIEUX — 1995-96
(14.63%)

In his penultimate NHL season, the Magnificent One played 709 games and beat out teammate Jaromir Jagr by 12 points, despite playing 12 fewer games than "Mario Jr."

## 7 WAYNE GRETZKY — 1989-90
(8.75%)

Gretzky's second year with the L.A. Kings saw him miss a number of games with minor injuries but he still finished 13 points ahead of his best friend and former teammate Mark Messier for the Art Ross, scoring 142 points. Messier had his revenge of sorts as the Oilers went on to win their fifth Stanley Cup of the decade.

## 6 CHARLIE CONACHER — 1933-34
(12.5%)

Despite missing half a dozen games during a short 48-game season, the high-scoring member of Toronto's famous Kid Line still finished six points ahead of Kid teammate Joe Primeau by scoring 52 points.

## 6 BERNIE GEOFFRION — 1960-61
(8.57%)

Boom Boom's first scoring title came the year he was the second man, after Maurice Richard, to score 50 goals in a season. His 95 points were five better than Habs' mate Jean Béliveau despite playing five fewer games. It was Geoffrion's second Art Ross after winning previously in 1954–55.

### 6    WAYNE GRETZKY — 1983-84
(7.5%)

Nothing could stop Gretzky in his prime, and although he missed a few games, he won the Art Ross by an astounding 81-point margin over second place point-getter Paul Coffey, his teammate in Edmonton. Remarkably, Gretzky could have stopped playing after his 42nd game and he still would have won the title.

### 6    MARIO LEMIEUX — 1996-97
(7.32%)

His last season in the league was a winning one for Lemieux. He finished 13 points up on Teemu Selanne of the Mighty Ducks to win the scoring title for the sixth time.

### 5    HOWIE MORENZ — 1930-31
(11.36%)

The Stratford Streak played five fewer games than Detroit's Ebbie Goodfellow but bested him by three points in the scoring race. Morenz then led his Canadiens to the Stanley Cup that year as well.

### 5    BOBBY HULL — 1965-66
(8.33%)

Hull became the first player to score more than 50 goals in a season, and his 97 points were a whopping 19 more than runner-up Stan Mikita who had played three more games.

# Ten **FEWEST CAREER GOALS** by Retired **1,000-GAME** Players

**1**

### BRAD MARSH — 23

Although he played in 1,086 regular season games, Marsh never scored more than three goals in any one season. In his rookie year, 1978–79, he went the entire season without a single goal. Twice more he played full seasons without scoring, but the highlight of his career was a goal in his only All-Star Game, in 1993.

**2**

### TERRY HARPER — 35

Harper played 19 NHL seasons and in 1975–76 scored a career-high eight goals for the Red Wings. He played the first ten years of his career with Montreal, winning five Stanley Cups as one of the team's top defensive players.

**3**

### DAVE LEWIS — 36

Three times did Lewis score five goals in a season with the Islanders, but he was unfortunate enough to be traded during the 1979–80 season, just weeks before the team began its run of four straight Cups. In 1,008 games, he also played for Los Angeles, New Jersey, and Detroit.

**4**

### HAROLD SNEPSTS — 38

A seven-goal man in 1978–79 with Vancouver, Snepsts was with the Canucks for most of 12 seasons. Twice he went an entire season without a goal, but in 1982 he was a +22 during the Canucks' drive to the Stanley Cup finals, where they lost to the New York Islanders.

**5**

### JEAN-GUY TALBOT — 43

After 17 years and seven Stanley Cups, Talbot averaged a goal every 25 games or so. He also had four more in 150 playoff games, again one of the lowest averages of all time, but his diamond-studded finger furniture more than made up for his poor shooting.

Brad Marsh heads up ice during the 1993 All-Star Game at the Montreal Forum.

## 6 GORD ROBERTS — 61

Roberts exploded onto the NHL scene with eight goals as a rookie with Hartford in 1979–80, but then settled into a defensive career which saw him score a total of just 61 goals in 1,097 games. During his six-team NHL career he also had the distinction of playing for three teams – Minnesota, Philadelphia, and St. Louis – during the '87–'88 season, and the culmination of his career came in the spring of 1992 when he helped the Penguins repeat as Cup champions.

## 7 JIM NEILSON — 69

Neilson spent the first 12 years of his NHL career with the Rangers, scoring a whopping ten goals in '68–'69. After playing for California and Cleveland, he went to the Edmonton Oilers for one final season of pro, 1978–79, the Oilers' last in the WHA.

## 8 LEO BOIVIN — 72

Although Boivin scored ten goals in 1963–64 with the Bruins, he was stationed on the Boston blueline most of his career and rarely became involved in offensive situations. Two years later, with two teams, he went the entire season without scoring, and in 19 seasons he averaged just over three goals a year.

## 9 MARCEL PRONOVOST — 88

Like Talbot, Pronovost won a handful of Stanley Cups in a defensive role. He played 16 years with the Red Wings during their four-Cup dynasty in the early 1950s, and then caught on with Punch Imlach's Over-the-Hill Gang in Toronto to win again in 1967 at the age of 37.

## 10 DOUG HARVEY — 88

Ironically, Harvey was called the Bobby Orr of his day, a great rushing defenseman who inspired Number Four when he joined the NHL. But Harvey's forte was to pass rather than score. He never had more than nine goals in even his best season, but he had 452 career assists, most of which came during the Original Six days. He also won the Norris Trophy seven times and the Stanley Cup six times.

# Nine **30-GOAL SCORERS** with the **FEWEST** Career NHL **GOALS**

### TOM WEBSTER — 33

**1**

A clever, offensive right-winger, Webster scored 30 times for the Detroit Red Wings in 1970–71. Injuries limited him to three goals in 12 games the next season and prior to the 1972–73 schedule, he signed with the New England Whalers of the WHA where he recorded 220 goals over six years.

### KEN HODGE JR. — 39

**2**

Apart from a splendid 30-goal rookie season, Hodge's NHL career was a disappointment. In 1991 he was a finalist for the Calder Trophy but was unable to keep his place in the league after that. Hodge, the son of the former Bruins great of the same name, eventually played in Britain and Germany before retiring in 1998.

### DIMITRI KVARTALNOV — 42

**3**

The Bruins chose this skilled left-winger in the first round of the 1992 Entry Draft. A few months later he was one of the club's top forwards with 30 goals and 72 points. In 1993–94, he slipped to 12 goals and spent much of the season in the American Hockey League. He later played in Switzerland and Austria before hanging up his skates in 1997.

### CHRIS VALENTINE — 43

**4**

A brilliant scorer with the Sorel Black Hawks of the QMJHL, Valentine was drafted in the 10th round by Washington in 1981. He began the 1981–82 season in the minors but was soon called up to the parent club where he accumulated 30 goals and 67 points. As the Caps improved in the mid-1980s, Valentine saw increasingly less ice time and eventually moved to West Germany where he excelled for a dozen seasons.

## 5 ROSAIRE PAIEMENT — 48

Scrappy centre Rosaire Paiement scored 34 goals for the expansion Vancouver Canucks in 1970–71. His output dropped to ten the next year and he eventually moved on to the WHA. In that league he recorded five 20-goal seasons while with the Chicago Cougars, New England Whalers, and Indianapolis Racers.

## 6 NIKOLAI BORSCHEVSKY — 49

The diminutive Siberian winger scored 34 goals for the Toronto Maple Leafs in 1992–93 then scored the overtime winner in game seven of the opening round playoff upset over the Detroit Red Wings. The next year he scored 14 goals but was hampered by a serious injury to his spleen. Borschevsky never returned to form and ended up skating in Europe by 1996.

## 7 KJELL DAHLIN — 57

Drafted out of the Swedish elite league, Dahlin scored 32 times for the Montreal Canadiens in 1985–86. He split the next two seasons between the Habs and the press box and left the NHL in 1988. Dahlin returned to play five more seasons with his old club, Farjestad, before retiring in 1993.

## 8 REG KERR — 66

A top scorer with the Kamloops Chiefs of the WCJHL, Kerr was originally drafted by the Cleveland Barons in 1977. He gained his first break as a pro with the Chicago Blackhawks where he was a useful role player for four seasons. He broke through with 30-goal season in 1980–81 but dropped to eleven the next season. He joined the Edmonton Oilers in 1983 but played chiefly with their AHL affiliate before retiring in 1984.

## 9 BOB CRAWFORD — 71

Crawford was a journeyman right-winger who plied his trade with four NHL organizations between 1979 and 1987. He enjoyed one excellent season for the Hartford Whalers in 1983–84 when he scored 36 goals. This proved to be his pinnacle in North America before he headed to Germany and Italy in 1987–88.

# Most **CAREER GOALS** without a
# **30-GOAL** Season

### 1 DALE HUNTER — 323

A hard-nosed centre for nearly two decades, Hunter played mainly with the Québec Nordiques and Washington Capitals. He reached the 20-goal mark nine times in his career but was best known for his playmaking and feisty leadership. Hunter totalled 688 assists and 3,446 penalty minutes to go along with his goal production.

### 2 AL MacINNIS — 301

Armed with one of the hardest shots in the league, defenseman Al MacInnis has scored more than his share of goals since joining the NHL on a full-time basis in 1983–84. He reached the 20-goal mark six times between 1987 and 1994, including a personal high of 28 on three occasions. In 1989, MacInnis won the Conn Smythe trophy after leading the Calgary Flames to the Stanley Cup and, in 1999, he was presented the Norris Trophy for the first time.

Blessed with one of the hardest shots in the NHL,
Al MacInnis topped the 300-goal mark during the
1999-2000 season.

**3** ## GEORGE ARMSTRONG — 296

One of the most consistent forwards in NHL history, Armstrong played every one of his 1,187 regular season games with the Toronto Maple Leafs. He hit the 20-goal mark four times but the closest he came to thirty was with 23 in 1959–60. "Chief" spent a team-record 21 seasons with the Leafs and captained them to four Stanley Cups in the 1960s.

**4** ## LARRY MURPHY — 285

A consistent offensive sparkplug throughout his career, Murphy developed into one of the top-scoring defensemen in NHL history. He was drafted fourth overall by the L.A. Kings in 1980 and promptly set an NHL record for rookie blueliners by amassing 76 points. He later won two Stanley Cups each in Pittsburgh and Detroit and posted five 20-goal seasons.

**5** ## DICK DUFF — 283

A charismatic and sharp-shooting left-winger, Duff was best remembered for his scoring exploits with the Maple Leafs and Canadiens. He recorded a career-high 29 goals in 1958–59 in addition to four other 20-goal performances. Duff played on two Stanley Cup teams in Toronto and four in Montreal and then moved on to L.A. and Buffalo before retiring in 1972.

**6** ## RED KELLY — 281

A terrific two-way defenseman for Detroit beginning in 1947, Kelly was moved to forward by coach Punch Imlach after Toronto acquired him in 1959–60. He recorded three consecutive 20-goal seasons from 1961 to 1963. One of the classiest stars in league history, Kelly was the first recipient of the Norris trophy in 1954 and was a four-time winner of the Lady Byng Trophy. He won four Stanley Cups each with the Wings and Leafs and was elected to the Hockey Hall of Fame in 1969 when the customary three-year waiting period was waived.

### 7 BOB PULFORD — 281

Pulford was an excellent checking forward who was capable of scoring his share of important goals. He reached the 20-goal mark four times including a personal-high of 28 in 1965–66. "Pully" helped Toronto win four Stanley Cups and scored a key overtime winner in the 1967 final versus the arch-rival Canadiens.

### 8 RALPH BACKSTROM — 278

Backstrom was a top amateur prospect of the Montreal Canadiens when the team began its run of five straight Cups in the mid-1950s. He joined the club in time to contribute to the last two of these and later played on four more championships with the Habs in the 1960s. Backstrom hit the 20-goal mark seven times in his career including a personal-best of 27 in 1961–62.

### 9 RON STEWART — 276

Stewart was one of the NHL's longest-serving performers. His career spanned 1,353 games in 21 seasons. The solid two-way centre helped the Toronto Maple Leafs win three straight Cups from 1962 to 1964. He generally hit double figures in goals scored but only twice did he reach the 20-goal plateau.

### 10 MURRAY OLIVER — 274

A fine playmaking centre who appeared in 1,127 regular season games, Oliver recorded five 20-goal seasons including three in a row for the Boston Bruins in the 1960s. He reached a personal-high of 27 for the Minnesota North Stars in 1971–72.

**1**

### WAYNE GRETZKY — 12

The "Great One" began his record string with 51 goals during his first NHL season in 1979–80. Along the way he totalled an NHL single season record of 92 in 1981–82 and five years he had at least 60. He scored 41 times for the Los Angeles Kings in 1990–91 before "slipping" to 31 the next season.

**2**

### MIKE BOSS — 9

One of the top pure goal-scorers in NHL history, Bossy reached the 50-goal mark in each of his first nine NHL seasons. His offensive talents were an integral part of the New York Islanders' four consecutive Stanley Cups from 1980 to 1983. A chronic back condition limited him to 38 goals in 1986–87, his last in the NHL.

**3**

### LUC ROBITAILLE — 8

Since joining the NHL in 1986–87, Luc Robitaille has been one of the league's most consistent scorers. That first year he scored 45 times and was presented the Calder trophy. He had at least 40 goals in each of his first eight seasons including a personal-high 63 in 1992–93. His string was ended by the NHL owners' lockout in 1994–95 when the season was reduced to 48 games.

**4**

### PHIL ESPOSITO — 7

Claiming the slot as his personal domain, Esposito was a goal-scoring machine throughout his 18-year career. Along with Bobby Orr, he was the key ingredient added to the Boston Bruins in the late 1960s that resulted in Stanley Cup championships in 1970 and 1972. "Espo" scored at least 40 times every year from 1968–69 to 1974–75. He retired in 1981 as one of the NHL's all-time leading scorers with 717 goals and 1,590 points.

### MICHEL GOULET — 7

**5**     Playing in an era dominated by the likes of Gretzky, Bossy, and Lemieux, Michel Goulet's brilliant career did not gain the acclaim it deserved. The first player ever drafted by the Québec Nordiques when they joined the NHL in 1979, Goulet lived up to the organization's dreams. His seven straight seasons with at least 40 goals came between 1982 and 1988.

### JARI KURRI — 7

**6**     Kurri's speed and quick release were the perfect complement to Wayne Gretzky's brilliant passes on the Edmonton Oilers of the 1980s. The two formed the NHL's most lethal offensive partnership with Kurri scoring at least 40 times from 1983 to 1989. The talented Finn also led all NHL playoff scorers four times and helped Edmonton win five Stanley Cups from 1984 to 1990.

**1**

## HECTOR BLAKE

Everyone knows him as "Toe" Blake, a nickname he got from his younger sister who called him "Hectoe." Eventually, the name was shortened to "Toe" and it stuck.

**2**

## ALEX LEVINSKY

Called "Mine Boy," Levinsky got his moniker because his father used to attend every game he played. He'd scream from the crowd, "That's mine boy!" and young Alex inherited the term.

Alex Levinsky inherited the nickname "Mine Boy" after his father continually exclaimed "That's mine boy!" when attending his games.

## 3 "TIM" HORTON

Horton's name is so well-known, few realize his real name was Miles. But his mother always called him "Tim" for short, as her nickname for him, and it became the name by which the outside world also called him.

## 4 JOHNNY BOWER

Bower played in the minors so long that he was jokingly referred to as the "China Wall" because of his longevity. The name was equally applicable to the NHL, though, because by the time he retired he was 45 and the oldest goalie ever to have played in the league.

## 5 TED KENNEDY

Like Blake, Kennedy's name comes from a sibling who pronounced Theodore, his given name, a little oddly. Theodore became "Teedore" and finally "Teeder," and he's been called that ever since.

## 6 GORDIE HOWE

Early in his career with Detroit, Howe was called "Winky" because he had a twitch in his eye that would begin unannounced and continue until it had run its course.

## 7 NELS STEWART

One of the toughest, meanest, dirtiest, and most talented players in the NHL's early days, Stewart was nicknamed "Ole Poison" for his various characteristics that made him fun to play with and a distinct displeasure to play against.

## 8 CLAIRE ALEXANDER

Even into the 1970s players often worked in the summertime. Alexander, a Maple Leaf, delivered dairy products during the off-season, and so he became known as the "Milkman."

### 9 JEAN BÉLIVEAU

Called "Le Gros Bill," Béliveau was the darling of Quebec society in the 1950s, first with the Quebec Aces and then the Canadiens in Montreal. His nickname originated from a popular French song of the day that goes by the same name and whose main character invoked the image of Béliveau.

### 10 DEREK SANDERSON

A lover of fast cars, women, and drink, "Turk" lived every day as if it were his last. His partying got the better of him – he lived like a Turk – and eventually ruined his career, but while he was with the Bruins he was winning Stanley Cups and living the high life. Ergo his nickname.

### **1** BERT LINDSAY — GOAL

Lindsay had a 1-3 record in the team's only four games of the season and could not find work again until the start of the next season, 1918–19. He signed with the Toronto Arenas and played most of the season, and then retired after having played in various pro leagues for the better part of a decade.

### **2** DAVE RITCHIE — DEFENSE

Ritchie played four games with the Wanderers before being claimed by the Ottawa Senators after the fire destroyed the Montrealers' home rink and forced the team to dissolve. He played in the NHL until 1926, but interrupted his career to try his hand as an official for three years in between.

### **3** PHIL STEPHENS — DEFENSE

He, too, played four games, then didn't resurface until 1921 when he played four more with the Canadiens. His odd pro career ended with 17 games with the Bruins in 1925–26 some nine years after his first stint in the NHL.

### **4** HARRY HYLAND — CENTRE

A Hall of Famer, Hyland also played only four games with the Wanderers and 13 with the Senators that year. His fame, however, came in the NHA, the predecessor to the NHL, where he played for the Wanderers for most of 1909–17.

### **5** BILLY BELL — LEFT WING

Bell played just 61 games in six NHL seasons, a fringe player mostly with the Canadiens. He scored just three goals and five points during his unspectacular career.

### JACK MacDONALD — RIGHT WING

**6**

MacDonald was claimed by the Canadiens and played t
next two years with the Habs. He joined the Quebec Bulldogs (wh
he had played for a number of years in the National Hockey
Association) for 1919–20 and played for Montreal and the Torontc
St. Pats over the next two seasons.

### JERRY GERAN — SUB

**7**

After one game with the Wanderers, it took Geran eight
years to get back into the NHL. He played in the United States
Amateur Hockey Association and spent a year in France, and then
joined the Bruins for 33 games in 1925–26.

### ART ROSS — SUB

**8**

Another Hall of Famer, Ross played just three career N
games, all with the Wanderers, but his contributions as a player
preceded the NHL. He played a dozen years and more in the NHA
and various pro teams in all parts of Canada, and of course went o
to become Boston's general manager and a pioneer in all facets of
the game.

### GEORGE O'GRADY — SUB

**9**

O'Grady was another graduate from the Wanderers of
the NHA, but after the NHL team folded he could find no work in
the NHL. These were his only four games in the league, after
which he retired from pro hockey altogether.

# FIVE PLAYERS Who Skated for All But One Original SIX TEAM

### 1 BRONCO HORVATH
(New York, Montreal, Boston, Chicago, Toronto)

A talented centre, Horvath's most productive years were in Boston where he hit the 30-goal mark twice including an NHL high 39 in 1959–60. He was selected to the NHL second All-Star Team in 1960. Horvath played nearly five years in the AHL before returning for 14 games with the expansion Minnesota North Stars in 1967–68.

### 2 HARRY LUMLEY
(Detroit, New York, Chicago, Toronto, Boston)

"Apple Cheeks" Lumley was one of the top goalies of the post-war period. His greatest years came with Detroit where he won a Stanley Cup in 1950 and led the NHL in victories twice and Toronto where he won the Vézina Trophy in 1954. Lumley retired in 1960 with career totals of 330 wins and 71 shutouts and was elected to the Hockey Hall of Fame in 1980.

### 3 VIC LYNN
(Detroit, Montreal, Toronto, Boston, Chicago)

Able to play defense and forward, Lynn wore all but the Rangers' uniform in the Original Six. He enjoyed his greatest period of success with the Toronto Maple Leafs' three straight Stanley Cup seasons from 1947 to 1949. He joined Boston in 1950–51 and recorded a career-high 14 goals before playing his last 40 NHL games with the Hawks in the Windy City.

### 4 BUD POILE
(Toronto, Chicago, Detroit, New York, Boston)

Poile spent the first half of his career in Toronto where he contributed to a Stanley Cup win in 1947 and played on the "Flying Forts" line with Gaye Stewart and Gus Bodnar. He scored 23 goals for Chicago after being involved in the largest NHL trade to that point, in November 1947. Poile also scored 21 goals for the Red Wings in 1948–49 and retired in 1950 with 229 career points.

### 5 GAYE STEWART
(Toronto, Chicago, Detroit, New York, Montreal)

Left-winger Stewart scored 24 goals as a rookie in 1942–43 and was presented the Calder trophy. After spending two years in the navy, he led the NHL with 37 goals in 1945–46 and helped Toronto win the Cup the next year. He and linemate Bud Poile were part of the blockbuster trade that brought Max Bentley to the Maple Leafs in the fall of 1947. Stewart rewarded the Hawks with 70 goals in three seasons. He retired in 1954 with career totals of 185 goals and 344 points.

# Ten **OBSCURE**
# **BROTHERS** in the NHL

**1**

### ANDY AND FRANK BATHGATE

Although Andy Bathgate had a Hall of Fame career in the NHL that lasted more than 1,000 games, his brother Frank wasn't so fortunate. Frank played Junior with the Guelph Biltmores for three years, and then moved on to the New York Rangers. But he played just two games with the Blueshirts in 1952–53, spending the rest of the season with Shawinigan in Quebec Senior hockey. He never made it back to the NHL, playing another decade in senior, primarily with the Windsor Bulldogs.

**2**

### DON AND DICK CHERRY

Although a famous tv personality, Don played just one NHL game, in the playoffs, for the Boston Bruins in 1955. His brother, Dick, fared only slightly better in a career that began with those same Bruins in '56–'57 for six games. Dick then spent many years in the minors and was not given another chance in the NHL until after expansion. He played for the Philadelphia Flyers for two full seasons, and then it was back to Senior hockey for the rest of his career.

**3**

### BOB AND BRAD GASSOFF

Bob was a regular with the Blues for four years in St. Louis, but his brother, Brad, had a less glamorous tour of duty with the Vancouver Canucks which drafted him in 1975. Over the next four years, he split his time between Vancouver and the farm in Tulsa with the Oilers, playing just 122 games in his NHL career.

## 4 JOHN AND DAN KORDIC

While Dan has established himself as a regular with the
Flyers during the 1990s, John's career was brief, explosive, and,
ultimately, tragic. Drafted by Montreal in 1983, John played for the
Habs from 1985 to 1989. But his role was clear and his temperament
suited to the team goon. He was traded to Toronto, and the Leafs
gave up on him because of erratic off-ice behaviour. He played with
Washington and Quebec, but one night in Quebec City he went on a
drug-induced, berserk riot and died while being restrained by a
number of the local constabulary.

## 5 STEVE AND JEFF LARMER

Steve Larmer played the vast majority of his 1,006 NHL
games with Chicago, but his younger brother, Jeff, had a less spectacular career with three teams over five years. Jeff scored 21 goals
with New Jersey in 1982–83, but that was as good as he would get.
After three unproductive seasons with his brother in the Windy
City, he spent a number of years in the minors before retiring.

## 6 ALAIN AND MARIO LEMIEUX

Mario was, of course, one of the greatest pure goal scorers
of all time, but few know he had an older brother in the league when
he joined Pittsburgh in 1984. Alain played with St. Louis for parts of
four seasons in the early '80s and even played a single game with
Mario and the Penguins in 1986–87. He was unimpressive, and this
turned out to be the last NHL game he ever played.

## 7 MARK AND PAUL MESSIER

"Moose" Messier is destined for the Hockey Hall of
Fame when he retires, but the same cannot be said for his brother,
Paul, who played nine games with the Colorado Rockies in
1978–79. Paul was drafted by Colorado out of the University of
Denver but spent a number of years in the minors before finishing
in Germany. He never played in the WHA and never played with
his brother.

### 8  DENIS AND JEAN POTVIN

Denis Potvin won four Stanley Cups with the dynastic New York Islanders in the early 1980s, but his brother Jean had perhaps the best career of this unknown group. Jean played eleven years in the NHL, the last two with the Islanders and the last, 1980–81, on the first Cup team. However, he never saw action in the playoffs and couldn't enjoy the victory celebrations with his brother.

### 9  LARRY AND MOE ROBINSON

One of the finest defensemen to play for the Canadiens, Larry Robinson was inducted into the Hall of Fame the moment he became eligible. His brother, Moe, however, played a single NHL game with his brother in Montreal. A defenseman as well, he was drafted by the Habs in 1977 and realized his dream during the 1979–80 season. His moment of glory was fleeting, however, and he finished the season in Nova Scotia with the farm team.

### 10  PATRICK AND STEPHANE ROY

Although Patrick Roy has won more than 400 games as an NHL goalie, brother Stephane played just 12 games with the Minnesota North Stars during the 1987–88 season. He scored one goal, but the rest of his career was a potpourri of international competition. Stephane played for Canada's national team, the World Junior team, and in Switzerland for four years.

### ROBBIE IRONS — 3

**1**

Irons played just three minutes in a game on November 13, 1968, replacing the great Glenn Hall and not allowing a goal for his brief stay with St. Louis and the NHL. He had been acquired from the Rangers with Camille Henry and Bill Plager for Don Caley and Wayne Rivers, but he never made any impression on coach Scotty Bowman and played the rest of his career in the International Hockey League.

Robbie Irons' NHL stats sheet consisted of three shutout minutes
played on November 13, 1968.

## 2  JEROME MRAZEK — 6

Mrazek allowed one goal during his half dozen minutes in the Philadelphia Flyers' goal during the 1975–76 season. A graduate of the University of Minnesota–Duluth and a Flyers' draft choice, he never played again in the NHL after this game.

## 3  JOE JUNKIN — 8

After playing eight minutes with the Bruins in 1968–69, Junkin suffered an horrific eye injury that cost him the whole of the '70–'71 season. He was never the same and never made it back to the big time, although he did have a brief career in the WHA for two years before retiring.

## 4  TOM McGRATTON — 8

McGratton was a spare goalie during an era when teams always carried just one main keeper. He replaced the injured Harry Lumley late in the game of November 9, 1947, for the Wings against the Leafs. He didn't allow a goal, but the Leafs still won handily, 6–0.

## 5  CORRIE D'ALESSIO — 11

D'Alessio came to Hartford in a trade that sent Kay Whitmore to Vancouver. Drafted 107th overall by the Canucks in 1988, his only NHL action was eleven minutes with the Whalers in 1992–93.

## 6  RICH PARENT — 12

Parent was undrafted and played most of his career in the IHL. He was signed as a free agent by St. Louis in the summer of 1997, but saw action in only one game, during the '97–'98 season.

**7** ### GREG REDQUIST — 13

Redquist was drafted 65th overall by Pittsburgh in the 1976 Amateur Draft after a four-year junior career with Hamilton and Oshawa in the OHL. The only game action he ever saw in the NHL came during the 1977–78 season when he allowed three goals in just 13 minutes of play. That was the alpha and omega of his NHL career.

**8** ### KEN BROWN — 18

Brown played junior hockey in Saskatchewan and then moved to the Central League in 1968. His only taste of the NHL came in 1970–71 with Chicago, and he allowed just one goal in his 18 minutes of glory. He went on to play two years with the Alberta/Edmonton Oilers in the WHA before leaving the pro game for good.

**9** ### JULIAN KLYMKIW — 19

A practise goalie with the Red Wings, Klymkiw played 19 minutes for the opposition Rangers in a Detroit–New York game on October 12, 1958, when the Blueshirts' own goaler, Gump Worsley, was injured early in the third period. Klymkiw managed to limit his Wings to just two goals against, but the Rangers still lost the game 3–0.

**10** ### JORDAN WILLIS — 19

Selected a distant 243rd overall in the 1993 draft by the Dallas Stars, Willis played all of 19 minutes with the big team durin the 1995–96 season, allowing one goal. Since then he has been in the IHL and is no longer Dallas property.

# Most Career Shutouts by a **GOALIE** Who **DEBUTED** after the **1967 EXPANSION**

### 1   TONY ESPOSITO — 76

"Tony O" took the NHL by storm in 1969–70 when he recorded fifteen shutouts for the Chicago Blackhawks and won the Calder and Vézina trophies. He continued to be one of the league's top netminders throughout the 1970s. Esposito hit double figures in shutouts a second time in 1973–74 when he shared the Vézina trophy with fellow Hall of Fame member Bernie Parent.

### 2   ED BELFOUR — 49

"Eddie the Eagle" was one of the top netminders of the 1990s. He made a bold entrance in 1990–91 by winning the Vézina, Jennings, and Calder trophies. Belfour led the NHL in shutouts four straight years from 1992 to 1995. In 1992 he helped Chicago reach the Stanley Cup finals and seven years later he backstopped the Dallas Stars to the first Cup triumph in franchise history.

### 3   PATRICK ROY — 48

During his rookie season in 1985–86, Roy elevated the Montreal Canadiens from a decent team to a Cup winner and was presented the Conn Smythe trophy. He became one of the dominant goalkeepers of his era, winning three Vézina trophies and twice leading the league in shutouts. Roy won a second Stanley Cup and Conn Smythe trophy with Montreal in 1993 and helped the Colorado Avalanche win their first championship in 1996.

### 4   KEN DRYDEN — 46

After winning the Conn Smythe and leading the Canadiens to the Stanley Cup in 1971, Dryden won the Calder trophy the following year, his first full year in the league. He went on to backstop Montreal to six Stanley Cups in the decade including four straight from 1976 to 1979. Dryden led the NHL in shutouts four times and registered a personal-high of ten in 1976–77.

## 5 DOMINIK HASEK — 45

A fine back-up in Chicago, Hasek got his big break when Buffalo starting goalie Grant Fuhr went down with a serious injury in 1993–94. "The Dominator" seized the opportunity by leading the league in shutouts and goals-against-average while earning the Vézina trophy. In the late 1990s he became the top goalie in the world by winning three more Vézina trophies and recording a remarkable 13 shutouts in 1997–98.

## 6 MARTIN BRODEUR — 42

Brodeur played his first full season for the New Jersey Devils in 1993–94 when he won 27 games and was the recipient of the Calder trophy. The following season he helped the team win its first Stanley Cup. During the late 1990s he solidified the Devils' position as a league power and won a personal-high 43 games in 1997–98. In 1996–97 and 1997–98 Brodeur recorded consecutive seasons of ten shutouts, and in 1999–2000 led New Jersey to a second Stanley Cup.

## 7 JOHN VANBIESBROUCK — 38

A consistent performer throughout his career, "Beezer" set a personal-high with six shutouts for the Philadelphia Flyers in 1998–99. Earlier he led the NHL in wins and won the Vézina trophy in 1985–86 as a member of the New York Rangers and helped the Florida Panthers reach the Stanley Cup finals in 1996.

## 8 TOM BARRASSO — 35

Drafted higher than any other American goalie, Barrasso proved the Buffalo Sabres right by winning the Calder and Vézina trophies in 1984. He later played with Pittsburgh and backstopped the team to consecutive Stanley Cups in 1991 and 1992 before being acquired by Ottawa at the NHL trade deadline in March, 2000.

### 9 CHRIS OSGOOD — 29

Osgood led the NHL with 39 wins and shared the
William Jennings trophy in 1995–96. In 1997–98 he led all goalies
with 16 playoff wins while helping Detroit repeat as Cup champions.
On March 6, 1996, he scored a goal against the Hartford Whalers.

### 10 ANDY MOOG — 28

Moog combined with Grant Fuhr to help the Edmonton
Oilers win the Stanley Cup in 1984, 1985, and 1987 before playing
with Boston, Dallas, and Montreal. Along the way he registered at
least 20 wins eleven times and was a respected team leader. In 1990,
he and teammate Réjean Lemelin won the Jennings trophy and led
the Boston Bruins to the Stanley Cup finals.

### 1   BAZ BASTIEN

Although he was developed in Conn Smythe's vaunted Toronto Marlies' system, Bastien did not pan out as the Maple Leafs had hoped. He played only five games at the start of the 1945–46 season when original replacement for Turk Broda – Frank McCool – was holding out for a better contract. After going winless in those five games, he never made it back to the NHL, and just three years later he suffered a serious eye injury at the Leafs' minor-league training camp that ended his career.

### 2   HARVEY BENNETT

Bennett played goal for almost 25 years, but only in the NHL during 1944–45 with the Boston Bruins. In 25 career games, he had a record of 10–12–2, allowing more than four goals a game. After the war he played another decade in the minors with the Bruins' AHL affiliate Providence Reds.

### 3   STEVE BUZINSKI

Nicknamed "The Puck Goes Inski" for good reason, Buzinski made it to the NHL only as a desperate replacement for the great Sugar Jim Henry. Buzinski surrendered almost six goals a game with the Rangers in 1942–43 for his nine games and after this season never played pro again.

After giving up nearly six goals per game during a brief stint with the Rangers in 1942-43, Steve Buzinski earned the moniker "The Puck Goes Inski."

## 4  MAURICE COURTEAU

While Sugar Jim Henry was playing for the Red Deer Army team during the war year of '43–'44, Courteau filled the breach for six unsatisfactory games, and like Buzinski gave up nearly six goals a game. His record of 2–4–0 earned him a trip to the minors, and he never returned to the NHL once the war ended.

## 5  CONNIE DION

One of the more successful war-time goalers, Dion survived two years and 38 games with Detroit from 1943 to 1945. He had a superb 23–11–4 record and a decent 3.11 goals against average, but after the war he spent nine years in the minors without being given another shot at the NHL.

## 6  HEC HIGHTON

Highton played for the Blackhawks in 1943–44, playing well in 24 games as a 20-year-old rookie. However, Mike Karakas was the team's goalie of the future and Highton was sent to the minors to play out the last years of his career.

## 7  SAM LOPRESTI

Prior to Karakas and after Chuck Gardiner in the Chicago goal, Lopresti lasted two seasons and 74 games with Chicago from 1940 to '42. He might well have been the goalie of the future, but he interrupted his career to enlist and when he came out he wasn't able to do any better than play for the San Diego Skyhawks of the Pacific Coast league.

## 8  FRANK McCOOL

Perhaps the greatest anomaly in this list, "Ulcers" McCool was fully the number one man in 1944–45 when Turk Broda was off at war. McCool played every game for the Leafs and took team to the Stanley Cup, recording three shutouts in the finals against the Red Wings. But he lasted the next year only until Broda returned to the team, and he was never heard of again, preferring retirement to a nerve-wrecking life of goaltending.

### 9   DOUG STEVENSON

He played only eight games between 1942 and 1946 as an injury replacement for Mike Karakas, and after the war Stevenson bounced around with umpteen teams and leagues for the next eleven years before calling it quits. He won only two of those eight games with the Hawks and let in almost five goals a game.

### 10   JOE TURNER

The first NHL casualty to the war, Turner played one game with the Red Wings in 1941–42 before going off to war. An American citizen, he was lost while serving with the U.S. Marine Corps in January 1945 at the age of 26, and the Turner Cup, emblematic of supremacy in the American League, is named in his honour.

# Most **PENALTY MINUTES** by a Player in His **ONLY NHL SEASON** (Original Six)

**1**   **D'ARCY COULSON — 103**

A graduate of the St. Michael's Majors in 1927, Coulson went on to play three years with the Ottawa Shamrocks in Senior hockey before joining the short-lived Philadelphia Quakers for the 1930–31 NHL season. In 28 games, he had nary a point, but visited the penalty box with regularity.

**2**   **FRANK PETERS — 59**

Peters kicked around the Can-Am league for a number of years before signing with the Rangers for 1930–31. Like Coulson, he didn't register a single point in his 43 career games during the season, only plenty of penalty minutes.

**3**   **PETER SLOBODIAN — 54**

A native of Dauphin, Manitoba, Slobodian played junior in Brandon and was given an NHL chance by the New York Americans. In his only season, he had five points to go with his 54 pims and the following year he began a successful career in various minor pro leagues in Western Canada.

**4**   **HAMBY SHORE — 51**

Shore's name on this list is a bit of a misnomer, for although he played only one season in the NHL, it was the league's first, 1917–18. Previously, he played a decade in the National Hockey Association (NHA), predecessor to the NHL, where he was a star with the old Ottawa Senators.

**5**   **JAMES HUGHES — 48**

Hughes played only during the '29–'30 season, with the Detroit Cougars. In 40 games, he had just one assist and the next year he was playing for the Olympics in Motown in minor pro. He played six years in the IAHL before retiring in 1936 at age 30.

### 6 WALT ATANAS — 40

Atanas had a long and peripatetic career, but in only on season, 1944–45, did he find himself in the NHL. This came durin the war when the Rangers, like all teams, were depleted by wartim enlistment by its players. Incredibly, he scored 13 goals in 49 game but the next season he was sent back to the American League whe he had been prior to joining the Blueshirts.

### 7 JOHN JACKSON — 38

Born in Windsor, Ontario, Jackson played for the Chicago Blackhawks during the 1946–47 season. In 48 games he had seven points, but he spent the vast majority of his eight-year hockey career in the United States Hockey League.

### 8 LIONEL HEINRICH — 33

Although little is known about Heinrich, he played for t Bruins in '55–'56 and in 35 games he had a goal, an assist, and 33 penalty minutes. He played for eight teams in six leagues during hi ten-year career before retiring in 1962.

### 9 VERN KAISER — 33

After playing for Springfield in the American League for two seasons, Kaiser was traded up to the NHL to the Canadiens for Charlie Gagnon in the summer of 1950. He made the team at training camp that fall and in 50 games with the Habs in the NHL the left-winger managed to score 12 points. Late in the season he was demoted to the farm team in Buffalo (the Bisons) and he never made it back to the big tent again.

# Most **POINTS** by a Player in His
# SOPHOMORE SEASON

**WAYNE GRETZKY**

164, 1980–81

Gretzky was considered ineligible for the Calder trophy in 1979–80 since he played in the WHA. He also conquered the "sophomore jinx" by breaking Phil Esposito's single season record with 164 points in 1980–81.

**MARIO LEMIEUX**

141, 1985–86

After winning the Calder trophy with a 100-point performance in 1984–85, Lemieux became a dominant NHL star in only his second full season. He recorded 48 goals and 93 assists while helping the Penguins improve by 23 points in the NHL standings.

**PETER STASTNY**

139, 1981–82

As a rookie, Stastny set a new rookie record with 109 points and won the Calder trophy. He followed this up with a thirty-point improvement and was a key figure in the Québec Nordiques' drive to the Stanley Cup semi-finals in 1982.

**KENT NILSSON**

131, 1980–81

A star with the Winnipeg Jets in the WHA, Nilsson scored 93 points for the Atlanta Flames in 1979–80. He followed that up with a personal best 49 goals and 82 assists when the team relocated to Calgary and reached the Stanley Cup semi-finals.

In 1980-81 Swedish star Kent Nilsson scored 131 points and helped th
Calgary Flames reach the semi-fina

### 5    MIKE BOSSY
126, 1978-79

Bossy set the NHL ablaze with a record 53 goals in a Calder
trophy performance in 1977–78. He met the challenge of topping
this by scoring league-high 69 goals in his second year.

### 6    DENIS SAVARD
119, 1981-82

A speedy centre with a host of tricky moves, Savard dazzled Chicago
fans with 75 points as a rookie on 1980–81. This was only the
beginning as he jumped into the category of legitimate star with a
44-point improvement in his second year.

### 7    MARK RECCHI
113, 1990-91

On the heels of a 30-goal rookie season, Recchi broke out with a
113-point performance in 1990–91. In the playoffs, he scored 34
points to help the Pittsburgh Penguins win the first Stanley Cup in
franchise history.

### 8    LUC ROBITAILLE
111, 1987-88

Robitaille scored 45 goals and won the Calder trophy in 1986–87.
The next year he took a further step forward by registering 53 goals
and 111 points while earning a spot on the NHL first All-Star Team.

### PIERRE LAROUCHE
111, 1975–76

Following a solid 31-goal rookie season, "Lucky Pierre" scored 53 goals and 58 assists and appeared to headed towards superstar status. He settled instead into the category of sometime star with 395 goals in 812 career games.

### 10 PAVEL BURE
110, 1992–93

Bure excelled as a rookie with 34 goals and the Calder trophy to his credit. The next year he burst through with his first of two straight 60-goal seasons while helping Vancouver set a franchise record with 101 points.

**1**

### WENDEL CLARK     13

Rarely has a player made such an impact on a city the way Clark did his first season in Toronto. A Calder Trophy competitor all year, he played in the 1986 All-Star Game but then didn't appear again until 1999 when he was a last-minute replacement. Playing before his hometown Tampa Bay Lightning fans, Clark was accorded the greatest ovation in the player introductions that year.

**2**

### DON BEAUPRE     11

Beaupre was a star goalie with the Minnesota North Stars in the early '80s and represented the team at the 1981 All-Star Game. He was the losing goalie for the Wales Conference, and didn't make it back to the big game until 1992 where he represented the Washington Capitals. In that game, he gave up six goals and was again the losing goalie of record.

**3**

### GUY LAFLEUR     11

Like Gordie Howe, there should be an asterisk beside his record. Lafleur played in six consecutive All-Star Games from 975 to 1980, but he retired in the mid-'80s for four years. In 1991, with the Nordiques, he was named to play in the game as the first Commissioner's selection. Thus, after Howe, he was the only man o play in the game after he had been inducted into the Hockey Hall of Fame.

**4**

### CHICO MAKI     10

Maki played in the 1961 All-Star Game as a member of the Cup-winning Hawks, and though he played his entire career with Chicago it wasn't until 1971 and '72 that he played again with the stars.

## 5  DALE HAWERCHUK  9

One of the leading point-getters during the high-scoring 1980s, Hawerchuk was team captain of the Winnipeg Jets and played at the All-Star Game five times that decade (including Rendez-vous '87). However, in a league with such depth at centre – notably Gretzky, Lemieux, and Yzerman – he didn't make it back to the All-Star Game until 1997 when he was added to the lineup via a Commissioner's selection.

## 6  BILL HICKE  9

Hardly a name synonymous with greatness, Hicke played in both the 1959 and '60 games as a member of the Stanley Cup-winning Montreal Canadiens. He never made it back until 1969 when he represented Oakland in the West Division, a naming that was due in large part to the fact that each team had to have one representative at the game.

## 7  GORDIE HOWE  9

A trick entry, of course, because almost every year Howe was in the league he was named to play in the "glitter game." However, during his hiatus in the WHA (1973–79), he was not eligible to play in the NHL's game. When the Hartford Whalers joined the NHL in 1979–80, Wales coach Scotty Bowman added him to the lineup, and in front of his adoring Detroit fans he received arguably the greatest ovation in All-Star Game history.

## 8  HARRY HOWELL  9

One of the greatest Rangers defensemen of all time, Howell represented the Broadway Blueshirts for the first time in 1954. Incredibly, he didn't play again with the stars until 1963 but then played in six of the next seven games.

# Eight **UNLIKELY MVPs** of the **ALL-STAR GAME**

**1**    **EDDIE SHACK**      **1962**

Shack was in the game only because he was on the Leafs' Cup-winning team, but he scored a goal late in the third period and livened up the game with his showmanlike skating. This was the first time the MVP award was handed out.

**2**    **BRUCE GAMBLE**      **1968**

This was an important game for a number of reasons. It was the last All-Star Game played at Maple Leaf Gardens and the first time since the game became an annual challenge that it was played at mid-season. The Leafs beat the All-Stars 4–3, and key to the victory was Gamble, who made 28 saves to become the first goalie to win the MVP.

**3**    **GREG POLIS**      **1973**

Named to the West Division team as the lone Pittsburgh representative, Polis nonetheless stole the award from Bobby Orr, Dave Keon, Jean Ratelle, and all the other greats in the game. He did so by scoring two goals, and it was the unlikeliness of the feat as much as its occurrence that prompted the media to give Polis the traditional MVP car.

**4**    **SYL APPS JR.**      **1975**

Injured at the last moment the previous year and unable to play, Apps's mere participation put him in the record books as the first son of a father to play in the All-Star Game. Captain Apps, Sr. of the Leafs had played in the '47 and '48 games, and dropped the ceremonial puck to the '49 contest. Like Polis two years previous, Apps was named MVP on the strength of his two goals.

### PETE MAHOVLICH          1976

With a goal and three assists, the Little M made history by becoming the first brother duo to both be named MVP at the game. Frank, the Big M, had copped the honour previously in 1969 as a member of the Red Wings. Pete did so while playing for the Wales Conference and representing the Canadiens.

### DON MALONEY          1984

Left-winger Maloney scored a goal – which turned out to be the game-winner – and assisted on three others to win the car. A member of the Rangers, this was his second consecutive, and last, All-Star Game appearance.

### GRANT FUHR          1986

During the highest-scoring decade of all, it was ironic that Fuhr stopped all 15 shots he faced from the Wales, notably Mario Lemieux, Mike Bossy, and Peter Stastny. Although the Wales went on to win the game in overtime, Fuhr's shutout period of play was good enough for him to be the acknowledged star of stars.

### MIKE RICHTER          1994

It's an improbable scenario that would see a goalie be named MVP in a game that ended in a 9–8 decision, but Richter played in net for the Eastern team and allowed just two goals on 21 shots, the lowest number allowed of all six goalers in the game. He became just the sixth goalie since 1962 to be named MVP.

# Ten Members of the **IIHF HALL** of **FAME** with North **AMERICAN** Connections

**1**

### VLADIMIR DZURILLA

Although he never played in the NHL, Dzurilla is most famous in North America as the goalie who came out of his net and committed too soon to Darryl Sittler in overtime of the Canada Cup finals in 1976. Sittler faked a shot and skated wide to shoot into the open net and give Canada victory. Dzurilla, though, played for Czechoslovakia in three Olympics and ten World Championships, winning a silver and two bronze in the former and three golds at the Worlds.

**2**

### ANDERS HEDBERG

Although Hedberg played his last pro years with the New York Rangers, he starred internationally with his native Sweden in 1969 as an 18-year-old. He won two silvers at the World Championships in 1970 and 1973 and a bronze in '72 and '74, and also played for Tre Kronor in both the '76 and '81 Canada Cup tournaments.

**3**

### HAKAN LOOB

After winning a Stanley Cup with the Calgary Flames in 1989, Loob moved back home to Sweden to continue his playing career. But prior to his arrival in the NHL, he also played for Tre Kronor in two Olympics and four World Championships and was a member of Sweden's gold medal team in Lillehammer in 1994, beating Canada in a shootout in the finals.

**4**

### SETH MARTIN

Martin played just 30 games in the NHL during the 1967–68 season for St. Louis as backup to the legendary Glenn Hall, but internationally he played goal for Canada in more games than any other man. He played in the 1964 Olympics in Innsbruck, and also in four World Championships during the 1960s when Father Bauer's National Team represented Canada abroad.

### VACLAV NEDOMANSKY

**5**      "Big Ned" played in both the WHA and NHL after defecting from Czechoslovakia, but previously he was that nation's finest forward. He was part of the 1972 World Championship team and he also won five silvers and three bronze medals at the WC. He also played in two Olympics, winning a silver in Grenoble in '68 and a bronze in Sapporo in '72.

### BORJE SALMING

**6**      Although Salming was one of the most popular players in Toronto Maple Leaf history during his 16 years on their blueline, "King" represented his native Sweden whenever he had the chance, beginning with the '72 and '73 WC. He played in three Canada Cups and, incredibly, also played at the 1992 Albertville Olympics at the age of 40.

Former Toronto hero Borje Salming played his last games at Maple Leaf Gardens while representing Sweden during the 1991 Canada Cup.

**7** HARRY SINDEN

Although Sinden never played in the NHL, his amateur career was enough to get him into the IIHF Hall of Fame. As defenseman and captain with the Whitby Dunlops, he led the team to the Allan Cup in both 1957 and '59 and in between the Dunnies won the World Championships in 1958 in Oslo. He also won a silver medal in the 1960 Olympics as an addition to the Kitchener–Waterloo Dutchmen who represented Canada that year in Squaw Valley.

**8** VLADISLAV TRETIAK

Regardless of nationality, league, era, or any other bias, Tretiak was simply one of the greatest goalies of all time. Although he was drafted by the Montreal Canadiens, he never played in the NHL. But his international career was unparalleled. He played in four Olympics and 13 World Championships starting at age 17, winning three gold medals in the Olympics and ten in WC play. He became known in North America for his exceptional play during the historic Summit Series on 1972, and he was the first Soviet-trained played inducted into the Hockey Hall of Fame.

**9** HARRY WATSON

Watson resisted all sorts of tempting offers to turn pro after his remarkable amateur career which culminated in 1924 with a gold medal at the first Olympic Winter Games. He scored an incredible 36 goals in the five games, including 13 in one contest against Switzerland in a 33–0 win. Leading up to the Olympics, Watson won two Allan Cups and three John Ross Robertson Trophies with the Toronto Granites and was considered far and away the best player not in professional hockey. After 1924, though, he retired from the game and went into business.

## 10 WILLIAM (W.A.) HEWITT

Father of legendary announcer, Foster, William was perhaps just as famous and important to hockey in his era as his son became a generation later. A journalist and editor, William was also secretary of the Canadian Amateur Hockey Association (CAHA) and travelled with the first two national teams to represent Canada at the Olympics, in 1920 and '24. He refereed the first Olympic hockey game ever played, and his judicious interpretations of the rules were so well admired that CAHA rules were immediately adopted as the official regulations for all international events for years to come.

# Ten LITTLE-KNOWN Members of the United States Hockey HALL OF FAME

### 1 EARL BARTHOLOME

Inducted into the US HHOF 1977, Bartholome spent his career in the minors with numerous teams, winning three Calder Cups with the Cleveland Barons in 1939, '41, and '45. His longest term of service was with the Barons, for which he played more than 500 games, a record for an American-born player in the American Hockey League.

### 2 JOE CAVANAGH

A New Englander by birth, he played three seasons with Harvard in the late 1960s and become one of their all-time point-getters before graduating. He won MVP awards in each year there, and was named to the ECAC's all-decade first All-Star Team. Since leaving the university, he has maintained an involvement in the game at the minor league level ever since.

### 3 JOE LINDER

Considered by many to be the first American star of hockey, Linder played for fifteen years near the start of the 20th century. He played for the Calumet Miners in 1905–06 in the International League, the first professional hockey league on the continent, and the following year played amateur hockey for five years in the Detroit area. In 1912 he moved to Minnesota where he was captain of Duluth in the American Amateur Hockey Association for eight years.

### 4 WALLY GRANT

Grant entered the US Hall in 1994 after a lifetime's involvement in the game. He played in the first-ever NCAA tournament in 1948 and in all played four seasons for the Michigan Wolverines between 1945 and 1950 (he was in the Army for one season). A member of the team's star "G Line" featuring Wally Gacek and Ted Greer, Grant won one NCAA title and played in three national tournaments altogether.

### 5 JACK KIRRANE

Kirrane had one of the more successful international careers for an American in the years following the war. He was named to the U.S. Olympic team for 1948 as a 17-year-old, but he never played in a game. He did represent his home and native land at both the 1957 and 1963 World Championships and played at the 1960 Olympics in Squaw Valley where the States beat both Canada and the Soviet Union to win the gold medal.

### 6 EDDIE OLSON

Olson's first brush with glory came during the war when he played with the Coast Guard Cutters, a team that featured NHLers Frank Brimsek and John Mariucci. After the war he played many years in the AHL, winning consecutive Calder Cups with the Cleveland Barons in 1953 and 1954.

### 7 BOB PARADISE

A member of St. Mary's College in Minnesota, Paradise turned down an offer from the Bruins to turn pro in order to finish his education and pursue a career as an amateur. He played for the U.S. at the 1968 Olympic Winter Games in Grenoble and at the World Championships the following year and finally turned pro with Minnesota for 1971–72. He played eight years in the NHL with four teams, playing a total of 368 games and scoring eight goals during those years.

### 8 TIM SHEEHY

Like Paradise, Sheehy pursued an education first before turning to professional hockey. He played three years at Boston College and then made the U.S. national team for 1969 where he stayed until after the 1972 Olympics. In Sapporo, he helped the U.S. win a stunning silver medal, and a few months later he signed with the New England Whalers of the WHA. He stayed in that league for six years and then spent three years in the NHL before retiring.

### 9 JOHN MATCHEFTS

A star with the University of Michigan who won three successive NCAA titles from 1951 to '53, Matchefts was a high-scoring forward in his playing days. Although he made the 1948 Olympic team, he never played at those Games. His first international experience came at the 1955 and '56 World Championships where he won a silver medal. He then became a high school coach and later coached Colorado College (1966–71) and the Air Force Academy (1972–86).

### 10 KEN YACKEL

After winning a silver medal with the U.S. at the Olympics in Oslo in 1952, Yackel played for the University of Minnesota Gophers before turning pro with Cleveland in the AHL. Three years later, while with the Providence Reds, he was called up to the Boston Bruins where he played his only six NHL games and later joined the Minneapolis Millers of the IHL. As a coach, he was behind the bench for the U.S. at the World Championships in 1965.

**1**

### DECEMBER 31, 1975

Montreal Canadiens 3    Central Red Army 3

During one of the great games ever played, the Habs outshot their Soviet opponents 38–13 but were forced to settle for a tie. Red Army netminder Vladislav Tretiak's brilliance conjured up images of the 1972 Summit Series.

**2**

### JANUARY 11, 1976

Philadelphia Flyers 4    Central Red Army 1

In the series finale, the defending Stanley Cup champions' intimidating style of play upset the Army to the point that they left the ice midway through the first period. When told they would not be paid, the Soviet officials quickly sent the club back onto the ice where they were outclassed and weary after a busy tour.

**3**

### JANUARY 4, 1976

Buffalo Sabres 12    Soviet Wings 6

In the most astonishing score of the Super Series, Richard Martin led the Sabres to a romp with two goals and three assists. The Soviets seemed confused as they ran into a team that was perfectly content to play a wide open and fast skating style.

**4**

### DECEMBER 28, 1975

Central Red Army 7    New York Rangers 3

In a flashback to the 1972 Summit Series, the Red Army debuted by shocking the hometown Rangers with their level of skill and polished attack. The winners were led by veteran forward Vladimir Petrov's four points and only two late New York goals prevented an even more embarrassing result.

**5** ## JANUARY 8, 1976
Central Red Army 5    Boston Bruins 2

Don Cherry's lunch-bucket crew found themselves up against a
patient and disciplined opponent. Boston outshot the Soviets 40 to
19 but found Tretiak virtually impenetrable. Valeri Kharlamov
scored twice as the Army remained undefeated in their first three
games of the tour.

**6** ## DECEMBER 29, 1975
Soviet Wings 7    Pittsburgh Penguins 4

Although clear subordinates to the powerful Red Army, the Wings
showed they were going to be a problem for any opponent by
defeating a Pittsburgh team that was highly regarded. Alexandre
Yakushev, Vladimir Shadrin, and Yuri Liapkin were the stars of this
squad that finished with a 3–1 record during the series.

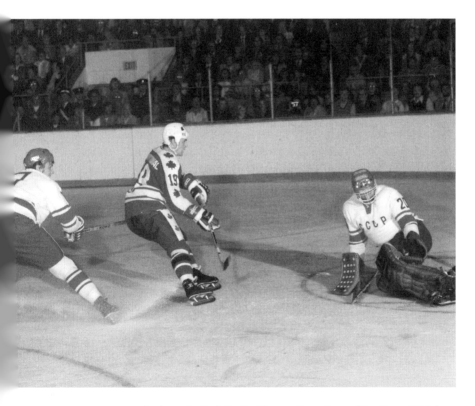

Soviet goalie Vladislav Tretiak wore the uniform of the Central Red Army
during the 1975-76 Super Series.

# Ten Best Players at the FIRST World
# JUNIOR CHAMPIONSHIPS in 1977

**1**

### JOHN ANDERSON

One of the pure goal-scorers on Canada that year, Anderson had ten goals in the tournament and like McCourt made the NHL that same year. Anderson joined the Leafs in Toronto and played eight years at Maple Leaf Gardens before moving on to Quebec and Hartford. Twice more he wore the red and white internationally, in the 1983 and 1985 World Championships.

**2**

### RON DUGUAY

Duguay was a flashy, charismatic player who developed great experience at these championships. He joined the Rangers at training camp in 1977, scoring 20 goals his first NHL season. The only other international games he ever played were in the 1981 Canada Cup, although after he retired from the NHL he played one season in Germany before returning to North America.

**3**

### VIACHESLAV FETISOV

One of the most internationally-decorated defensemen of all time, Fetisov began his illustrious career at age 17 here at the WJC. He was voted the tournament's best defenseman and went on to play in eleven World Championships as well as three Olympics and two Canada Cups. All of this he accomplished before joining the NHL and playing 546 games with North America's best.

**4**

### PETER IHNACAK

Ihnacak was one of the best players for the Czech team that won the bronze medal in his native land that hosted the WJC. After the WJC, he played five years in the Czech league before defecting and coming to Toronto to play for the Leafs. After eight years with the Blue and White, he resumed his career in Europe, notably in Germany and Switzerland.

## 5   SERGEI MAKAROV

A teammate of Fetisov's on the gold medal Junior team, Makarov had an equally successful international career with CCCP, representing his country in every major tournament from 1977 to 1989 when he became one of the first Soviets to join the NHL. He played seven seasons with Calgary, San Jose, and Dallas, and then moved back to Moscow to play two years in Russia before retiring.

## 6   DALE McCOURT

One of the emerging superstars from the '77 WJC, McCourt led Canada in scoring with 18 points in seven games en route to a silver medal. That same fall he made the Red Wings as an 18-year-old and played only twice more, at the WC, for Canada internationally. After 532 NHL games, he moved to Europe in 1984 and had another successful seven-year career with Ambri Piotta in the Swiss League.

## 7   MATS NASLUND

Although Naslund and his Swedes finished fifth at the 1977 WJC, he had a long and proud career both with Tre Kronor and the Montreal Canadiens, playing for the former from 1977 to 1982, and then the Habs for eight seasons. Naslund returned to Europe to play for four years and then returned to the NHL, with Boston, for the end of the 1994–95 season at the age of 35.

## 8   ROB RAMAGE

Ramage had just one assist for Canada in 1977, but he developed into a complete defenseman in the NHL who could skate, hit, and fight when need be. He played more than 1,000 games in the NHL and played in the 1978 WJC and the WC in 1981 after his Colorado Rockies failed to make the playoffs. He played for eight teams during his career, finishing with Philadelphia in '93–'94.

## 9 REIJO RUOTSALAINEN

A native of Finland, Ruotsalainen had a distinguished international career before moving to North America in 1981. He played in three WJC's altogether, and in 1979 completed the rare double of playing both the Junior and World Championships in the same season. He also played in the 1981 Canada Cup and 1988 Olympics in Calgary.

## 10 RIC SEILING

A quiet and unassuming player, Seiling nonetheless had good hands and a scorer's touch around the net. He had three goals for Canada in Czechoslovakia in '77 and with Buffalo he went on to produce four straight 20-goal seasons. The WJC was the highlight of his international career.

# Seven **LONGEST** Last **NAMES**
## of Active Players

### 1 JAMIE LANGENBRUNNER
13 LETTERS

Langenbrunner was drafted by Dallas in 1993 and has been with
the Stars ever since. A native of Minnesota, he was a member of
the 1999 Stanley Cup team and also represented the United States
at the 1998 Olympic Winter Games in Nagano, Japan.

### 2 RYAN VANDENBUSSCHE
13 LETTERS

Although he was drafted by Toronto in 1992, Vandenbussche never
played a game for the Blue and White. Instead, he was signed as a
free agent by the Rangers but after just 27 games over two years he
was traded to Chicago where he has been ever since.

Forward Jamie Langenbrunner helped the Dallas Stars win their first Stanley Cup in 1999.

### 3  JOHN VANBIESBROUCK
13 LETTERS

The only goalie among this select group, the "Beezer" has more than 350 NHL wins. He has eight seasons of 20 or more wins, and in 1985–86 led the league with 31. After eleven seasons with the Broadway Blueshirts, he played for Florida and then the Flyers.

### 4  HNAT DOMENICHELLI
12 LETTERS

Although he has yet to break into the NHL full-time, Domenichelli has played for Hartford and Calgary after being drafted by the Whalers in 1994. After playing four years with the phenomenal Kamloops Blazers team that won three Memorial Cups in four years, he has spent most of the last few years in the American Hockey League.

### 5  GLEN FEATHERSTONE
12 LETTERS

A native of Toronto, Featherstone has been in the league since 1988 with five different teams. A defensive defenseman, he has scored but 19 goals in 384 games. In nine NHL seasons, he played just 28 playoff games.

### 6  PETE LeBOUTILLIER
12 LETTERS

A native of Manitoba, LeBoutillier played junior for Red Deer and was drafted by the Mighty Ducks of Anaheim in 1995. He was one of only a few players to have been drafted twice, having been originally selected by the Islanders in '93. Unsigned in two years, he went back into the draft and has been a part-time player with the Ducks ever since.

### 7  VADIM SHARIFIJANOV
12 LETTERS

Born in Ufa, Soviet Union, in 1975, Sharifijanov has played with the New Jersey Devils since 1996 after being drafted 25th overall two years previous by the team.

# Eight SHORTEST LAST NAMES
## of GOALIES in NHL History

**1**

### ABBIE COX

Cox played only five games between 1929 and 1936 with four different teams, but his wasn't a brief pro career. He was a staple in the IAHL for many years and came up to the NHL to replace injured goalies on each occasion.

**2**

### CLAUDE CYR

Cyr played only one period in the NHL, for the Montreal Canadiens, to replace Claude Pronovost on March 19, 1959. He won a gold medal with the Trail Smoke Eaters for Canada at the 1961 World Championships and played for a number of years in the Quebec Senior League, but otherwise his pro career was brief and without fanfare.

**3**

### PETER ING

Ing became the number-one goalie for the Toronto Maple Leafs in 1990–91 but was traded to Edmonton in the blockbuster deal that saw the Leafs acquire Grant Fuhr. Ing played just 12 games with the Oilers and three with Detroit in 1993–94 before finishing his career in the IHL.

**4**

### RON LOW

One of the more successful short-name goalies, Low played in the NHL for eleven years with six teams before becoming the Oilers' head coach for four seasons. His record was 102–203–38, and his goals against a generous 4.28.

**5**

### DARRELL MAY

May appeared in just six games in the NHL, all with St. Louis from 1985 to 1988. He played the majority of his pro career with the Peoria Rivermen of the IHL and he retired at age 27 having won but one game in the NHL.

### 6   EDDIE MIO

Drafted 174th overall by Chicago in 1974, Mio is part of a trivia answer in that he was involved in the trade that sent Wayne Gretzky from Indianapolis to Edmonton (along with Peter Driscoll). Mio played in the WHA with the Edmonton Oilers and stayed with the team when they joined the NHL in 1979. He also played for the Rangers and Detroit, and in all played 192 NHL games.

### 7   JAMIE RAM

One of the lowest draft choices to make it to the NHL, Ram was selected 213th overall by the Rangers in 1991. But Ram's chance in the big leagues lasted all of 27 minutes in 1995–96. He didn't allow a goal, but with Mike Richter the number-one man in Manhattan he wasn't given much of a chance and he has been in the minors ever since.

### 8   PATRICK ROY

The most likely Hall of Famer in this group, Roy ranks statistically among the greatest goalies ever in terms of games played, minutes played, and victories. He has won three Stanley Cups and two Conn Smythe Trophies, and eight times he has won more than 30 games in a season.

# Ten Best Players Whose **LAST NAME STARTS** with a **"V"**

### 1 ROGIE VACHON

The 5'7" Vachon was an inspiration to diminutive netminders all over North America while recording 355 wins and 51 shutouts in the NHL. He played his first five seasons with the Montreal Canadiens where he helped the club reach the Stanley Cup finals in 1967 and win the title in 1968 and 1969. In 1971, Vachon was traded to the L.A. Kings where he enjoyed his finest years with nine, 20-win seasons. In 1976, he was selected Team MVP when he backstopped his country to the inaugural Canada Cup title.

### 2 CAROL VADNAIS

Blessed with fine offensive instincts, Vadnais played both left-wing and defence. He began his NHL career with the Montreal Canadiens before joining the expansion Oakland Seals in their sophomore year of 1968–69. Vadnais scored a personal-high 24 goals in 1969–70 and later joined the Boston Bruins. He helped the Bruins win the Stanley Cup in 1972 and, in 1975, was part of the block-buster trade with the Rangers that involved Phil Esposito and Jean Ratelle.

### 3 RICK VAIVE

Vaive utilized his speed, blazing shot, and combative will to become one of the NHL's top goal-scorers in the 1980s. He began his pro career in 1978–79 as one of the 18-year-old "Baby Bulls" on the Birmingham franchise in the WHA. After that league disbanded, the Vancouver Canucks drafted him 5th overall in 1979. A trade in February 1980 brought Vaive to Toronto where he became the first Maple Leaf to record a 50-goal season.

## 4 JOHN VANBIESBROUCK

One of the top goalies ever produced in the United States, Vanbiesbrouck enjoyed a superb amateur career with the Soo Greyhounds of the OHA/OHL before joining the New York Rangers on a full-time basis in 1984–85. After leading the NHL with 31 wins in 1985–86 he was presented the Vézina Trophy. In 1993, he was the first player chosen by the Florida Panthers in the expansion draft. Two seasons later, "Beezer" guided the team all the way to the Stanley Cup final and later signed with the Philadelphia Flyers as a free agent.

## 5 JOHN VAN BOXMEER

A fine playmaking defenseman, Van Boxmeer began his NHL career in the Montreal Canadiens' organization. Unable to gain adequate playing time with the powerful Habs, he joined the Colorado Rockies in 1976–77 where he became a stalwart on their blueline. In 1978, he scored 54 points on a weak Rockies team and later played a key offensive role for the Buffalo Sabres.

## 6 PAT VERBEEK

Combining toughness and scoring, Verbeek became one of the most consistent forwards in the NHL since debuting in 1983–84. During the 1980s he was one of the few bright lights on a poor New Jersey Devils squad. In 1987–88, he scored a personal best 46 goals and helped the team reach the playoff semi-finals. He later played for Hartford, the New York Rangers, and Dallas where his tenacity was key ingredient in the latter's first-ever Stanley Cup triumph in 1999.

## 7 MIKE VERNON

A native of Calgary, Alberta, Vernon provided excellent goalkeeping in his hometown with the junior Wranglers before making his NHL debut with the Flames. He was Calgary's starter between 1987 and 1994, recording four, 30-win seasons and helping the franchise win its first Stanley Cup, in 1989. In the summer of 1994 he was traded to Detroit where he won the Conn Smythe Trophy by leading the team to the Stanley Cup in 1997.

## GEORGES VÉZINA

One of hockey's all-time greatest netminders, Vézina starred for the Montreal Canadiens in the NHL and its precursor, the National Hockey Association. His coolness under fire earned him the nickname "the Chicoutimi Cucumber" while his superb ability helped the Montreal club win five league titles and two Stanley Cups. Vézina's career ended tragically at the start of the 1925–26 season when tuberculosis left him unable to play. He died just a few months later and in 1945 was among the first twelve inductees to the newly founded Hockey Hall of Fame.

Legendary goaltender Georges Vézina was one of the twelve inaugural inductees to the Hockey Hall of Fame in 1945.

### 9  STEVE VICKERS

A solid left-winger with a gifted scoring touch, Vickers entered the NHL in style in 1972–73 by scoring 30 goals and winning the Calder Trophy. He went on to score at least 30 goals four times and contributed to the Blueshirts' drive to the Stanley Cup finals in 1979. The classy Vickers enjoyed his finest year in 1974–75 scoring 41 times and earning selection to the NHL's second All-Star Team. He retired in 1982 with 246 career goals to his credit.

### 10  CARL VOSS

A solid all-around centre, Voss played 261 NHL games for eight different teams from 1927 to 1938. In 1933, he enjoyed a fine rookie season with the Detroit Red Wings and was the first recipient of the Calder Trophy. Just before retiring in 1938, he scored the Cup-clinching goal to bring the Chicago Blackhawks their second Stanley Cup. After retiring as a player he remained in hockey and became one of the most respected referees-in-chief in NHL history.

# Ten **SURNAMES** with **AN X**

**1**

### P.J. AXELSSON

A three-year veteran of the Bruins, Per-Johan played his junior hockey for Vastra Frolunda in Sweden before joining Boston for the '97–'98 season.

**2**

### RANDY EXELBY

Born in Toronto, Exelby played one game in goal for Montreal in '88–'89 and another for Edmonton the following year after being traded for future considerations. In fact, his stint lasted just three minutes with the Habs, and although he played the full game with the Oilers he allowed five goals in a losing cause. He never played in the NHL after that.

**3**

### WAYNE GROULX

Drafted a lowly 179th overall by the Quebec Nordiques in 1983, Groulx played exactly one game in the NHL, in '84–'85, after four years with the Soo Greyhounds in the OHL. He spent the rest of his career in the minors and later Europe, and although he was born in Welland, Ontario, his dual citizenship allowed him to play for Austria at the World Championships on two occasions.

**4**

### ORVILLE HEXIMER

Nicknamed "Obs," Heximer played for three NHL teams in three seasons during the 1930s, and only once a full season, with Boston, in 1932–33. A small forward, he spent most of his career in the minors and in Senior hockey, but he did score 13 goals in 84 NHL games.

**5**

### GASTON LEROUX

A native of Montreal, Leroux played exactly two games in the NHL with his hometown Canadiens during the 1935–36 season. He didn't register a point, and for the rest of the decade before and after he played minor pro almost exclusively in Quebec.

## 6 CHRISTIAN PROULX

Like Leroux, Proulx was born in Quebec and played his only games, seven in all, with the Canadiens. He had a goal and two assists during his promotion from Fredericton of the AHL but never played in the NHL after that brief time at the Forum.

## 7 GERRY RIOUX

A free agent signed by Winnipeg, Rioux played just eight uneventful games with the Jets during the 1979–80 season, the team's first in the NHL after joining the league from the WHA. After just one more season of pro, he retired in 1981.

## 8 FLORENT ROBIDOUX

Robidoux was born in Manitoba and played junior in the Western league. He was undrafted, but played 52 games in the NHL all with Chicago during three call-ups from the minors between 1980 and 1984, after which he went to the IHL for the rest of his career.

## 9 RICK ST. CROIX

A career backup goalie, St. Croix played only for Philadelphia and Toronto during his 129-game NHL career between 1977 and 1985. Only twice did he play in more than 20 games a season and only once, in '80–'81, did he play more than one game in the playoffs.

## 10 JOHN VAN BOXMEER

In 1974, Montreal had four of the first 14 draft choices, and with their last of those they selected defenseman Van Boxmeer, a native of Petrolia, Ontario. He played parts of four seasons with Montreal before being traded to Colorado, and during his eleven years in the league he scored more than 50 points four times.

**1**

### AL ARBOUR

Although his name suggested that liberal use of the lumber was part of his repertoire, Arbour was a clean player who relied on discipline and solid positional play to succeed. He played 626 games with four different teams and won the Stanley Cup with Chicago in 1961 and Toronto the next year.

**2**

### DON BIGGS

Contrary to his surname, the skilful centre stood only 5'8" and failed to earn a regular place in the NHL during the 1980s. He played briefly with Minnesota and Philadelphia but was primarily a veteran of the AHL and IHL.

**3**

### ANDRÉ CHAMPAGNE

A career minor league left-winger, Champagne played two games for the Toronto Maple Leafs while the team was in the midst of three straight Cup wins from 1962 to 1964. He did not factor in the team's plans however and consequently missed out on being sprayed with the bubbly at the end of the season.

André Champagne played two games for the Maple Leafs during their glory years but was never on hand to sip the "bubbly."

### 4 REG NOBLE

Although his skill level on the ice was superior, Noble was hardly a role model after the game. He was notoriously rebellious wherever he played, often favouring socializing over practices. The notion of a nightly curfew was often deemed insulting to him. His talent was such that teams put up with his antics because he helped them win games.

### 5 RICH PILON

Although not the swiftest player in the league, Pilon gained a full-time NHL place because of his rugged play and solid positioning on the ice. Enemy forwards were always aware of his presence when going on the attack. Pilon's veteran leadership helped the New York Islanders reach the Stanley Cup semi-finals in 1992–93.

### 6 LARRY PLAYFAIR

A rugged 6'4" defenseman, Playfair patrolled his zone over 688 games from 1978 to 1990. Rather than treating the opposition fairly, he adopted a rugged approach to dealing with enemy skaters. Seven times he exceeded 150 penalty minutes and finished with 1,812 career minutes served.

**1**

**BEHN**

A fierce defenseman who teetered between physical and goon-like in his play, Behn was taken 6th overall by the Flyers in 1978. He had size and some offensive skills, but his was an intimidating presence on the ice. He was suspended numerous times during his career for various stick and fist violations and retired after '87–'88 with injuries that prevented him from playing such a physical game any longer.

**2**

**BERT**

As a left-winger, Bert played for four teams during his 478 games in the NHL in the 1970s, staying with Los Angeles for four and a half of those years. He never scored more than nine goals in a season but twice hit the century mark in penalty minutes.

**3**

**CAREY**

Although he was drafted by Chicago, Carey was traded to Calgary and it was as a Flame he began his NHL career. He scored 20 goals in each of his first three full seasons as a forward and also played for Hartford and the Rangers before returning to the Flames for the final three years of his career, 1990–93. He missed Calgary's Stanley Cup run in 1989, and in ten seasons played in only 52 playoff games.

**4**

**CULLY**

Carol "Cully" Wilson played for many years in the Pacific Coast league before joining the NHL with the Toronto St. Pats in 1919. He played 125 games with the new league but scored 59 goals before returning to lesser pro leagues in North America. Although he never won a Stanley Cup, his pro career in all lasted some twenty years.

**5**

### DOUG

A 16-year veteran of the NHL, 14 with Chicago, Wilson was one of the finest offensive defensemen of his era. In 1981–82 he scored 39 goals from the blueline, the same year he won his only Norris Trophy. He also played in seven All-Star Gamess and finished his career with the expansion San Jose Sharks.

**6**

### JOHNNY

A veteran of 688 games during the golden age of Original Six, Johnny played for four of those teams – Detroit, Toronto, Chicago, and the Rangers. A gentlemanly player, he had only 66 penalty minutes during a career which culminated in consecutive Cups with Detroit in 1954 and '55.

**7**

### LARRY

This Wilson played just two full seasons in the NHL and parts of four others with Detroit and Chicago, but he skated for 13 years with the Buffalo Bisons in the American League after he was no longer wanted by the NHL.

**8**

### LEFTY

A trainer for Detroit for decades, Lefty was famous for filling the breach on a number of occasions when a goalie was injured and a quick replacement had to be found. He played for his Wings one night, but twice he actually played against his mates, including a 52-minute stint with the Bruins. He allowed just one goal in a 2–2 tie after Don Simmons, the starter, was hurt early in the game.

**9**

### MURRAY

Although not the most-skilled left-winger in the 1970s, Murray was fortunate enough to play for Montreal and thus won three Stanley Cups. Drafted a high 11th overall, he only once scored more than 20 goals in a season, and after six years with the Habs he finished his career playing for Los Angeles for one season.

## 10 RON

A native of Windsor, Ron is better known for playing in Europe and representing the United States internationally than he is for anything Canadian. He played parts of his first three years in the NHL with the Leafs, but then moved to Switzerland and later played at the World Championships for the U.S. After retiring in 1988, he turned to coaching and won the World Cup in 1996 with the American team before placing a disappointing sixth at the 1998 Olympic Winter Games with more or less the same team.

### 1   CRAIG LUDWIG    (13 YEARS)

A solid stay-at-home defenseman, Ludwig helped the
Montreal Canadiens win an unexpected Stanley Cup in 1986.
During his last NHL season in 1998–99 he was part of the Dallas
Stars' first Stanley Cup triumph. He retired after the victory having
played 1,256 NHL games.

### 2   BRIAN SKRUDLAND    (13 YEARS)

A solid defensive centre, Skrudland scored a key overtime
goal when the Canadiens won the Stanley Cup in his rookie season
in 1985–86. He later helped the Florida Panthers reach the finals in
1996 and was a veteran leader on the Dallas Stars' first Cup triumph
in 1998–1999.

### 3   MARCEL PRONOVOST    (12 YEARS)

Pronovost was an integral member of the Detroit Red
Wings' blueline corps when they defeated the Montreal Canadiens
in a bitter seven-game final in 1955. He was on hand again in 1967
when the Toronto Maple Leafs downed the Habs in a six-game
final during Canada's centennial year.

### 4   TERRY SAWCHUK    (12 YEARS)

Sawchuk backstopped the Red Wings to their third
Stanley Cup in four years in 1955. Many claim his netminding in the
early 1950s was the best ever seen. In 1967 he showed flashes of his
former brilliance by combining with Johnny Bower to help Toronto
win its fourth Stanley Cup of the decade.

### 5   GREG GILBERT    (11 YEARS)

As a rookie, Gilbert helped the New York Islanders sweep
the Edmonton Oilers to win their fourth straight Stanley Cup in
1983. Prior to the 1993–94 season, his veteran savvy was sought by
the New York Rangers. A few months later, he played an important
checking role on the club's first Stanley Cup triumph in 54 years.

## 6 JOE NIEUWENDYK (10 YEARS)

In Nieuwendyk's first two NHL seasons with the Calgary Flames he won the Calder trophy in 1988 and the Stanley Cup the next year. He was traded to Dallas in December 1995. Four years later, he won the Conn Smythe trophy after leading the Stars to their first-ever Stanley Cup.

Joe Nieuwendyk won the Stanley Cup with the Calgary Flames
in 1989 and Dallas Stars in 1999.

# Seven Least-Known Players to **SCORE** a **CUP-WINNING** Goal

 **PETE BABANDO**
Detroit Red Wings, 1950

A journeyman forward who played on four different clubs, Babando scored 86 regular season goals along with three in the post-season. Of his trio of playoff goals, none was bigger than the overtime winner in the seventh game of the finals versus the New York Rangers. This was the first extra period winner ever scored in a game seven.

 **JOE CARVETH**
Detroit Red Wings, 1943

A solid NHL right-winger, Carveth registered three 20-goal seasons playing for the Red Wings, Bruins, and Canadiens in the 1940s. His moment of glory came in 1943 when he scored the goal that brought Detroit the third Stanley Cup in franchise history. Carveth opened the scoring in the Wings' 2–0 win which completed a four-game sweep over the Boston Bruins.

 **REG FLEMING**
Chicago Blackhawks, 1961

The Chicago Blackhawks' only Cup-clinching goal of the last half of the twentieth century was not scored by one of its big name stars. Rookie enforcer Reg Fleming was credited with the second Hawks goal when they defeated Detroit by a 5–1 score to take the Cup in six games.

 **PETE KELLY**
Detroit Red Wings, 1936

Kelly was a useful role player from the right-wing who scored one huge playoff goal in his career. It came in the fourth game of the finals and gave the Wings a 3–2 win over Toronto and 3–1 victory in the best-of-five series. Kelly only scored three goals in 19 playoff games but picked a useful time to come through on April 11, 1936.

## 5 BOB KELLY
### Philadelphia Flyers, 1975

One of the toughest members of the Flyers' "Broad Street Bullies," Kelly scored 154 goals in twelve NHL seasons. His biggest playoff moment came at the expense of the Buffalo Sabres when he scored the first goal in Philly's 2–0 win in game six of the 1975 final. The win gave the Flyers their second straight Stanley Cup.

## 6 PETE LANGELLE
### Toronto Maple Leafs, 1942

Langelle spent only three full seasons in the NHL and scored a mere five goals in 41 playoff games. He carved a place in history on April 18, 1942, when his winning goal completed Toronto's stunning comeback from being down three games to none against Detroit to win the Cup.

## 7 WAYNE MERRICK
### New York Islanders, 1983

Merrick was a first-rate checking centre who became an important role player on the New York Islanders' four straight Stanley Cup triumphs in the early 1980s. On May 21, 1981, his goal stood as the winner when the Isles defeated Minnesota 5–1 to win the series four games to one.

# Seven Largest **POINT DECREASES** by a Team in **ONE SEASON**

### 1 — **DETROIT RED WINGS**
1970-71 (-40)

During the 1969–70 season, the Wings featured the top scoring line in hockey of Alex Delvecchio-Gordie Howe-Frank Mahovlich. They won 40 games and finished with 95 points before losing to Chicago in the quarter-finals. The next year, Mahovlich was traded and Howe was playing his last year. The team won only five of 39 games on the road and dropped to 55 points and a seventh place finish in the East Division.

### 2 — **CHICAGO BLACKHAWKS**
1953-54 (-38)

The 1952–53 season was a blip on an otherwise dismal screen in the history of the Hawks. The club finished within one game of .500 and made the playoffs for the only time in a twelve-year period. The next season they dropped to 31 points and again failed to qualify for the post-season.

### 3 — **WINNIPEG JETS**
1985-86 (-37)

In 1984–85, the Jets enjoyed their finest NHL season with 95 points. Star centre Dale Hawerchuk scored 130 points, coach Barry Long finished runner-up in the voting for the Jack Adams Award, and the team even won a playoff round before their customary exit courtesy of the Edmonton Oilers. The following season the Jets dropped to 59 points and didn't even have a winning record on home ice.

The Detroit Red Wings won their first Stanley Cup in 42 years in 1997 then repeated their feat in 1998.

### DETROIT RED WINGS
1996-97 (-37)

The Wings dominated the NHL regular season in 1995–96 with 62 wins but ultimately disappointed their fans by losing to Colorado in the Western Conference final. The next season they paced themselves and finished with 94 points. More importantly, they saved their best hockey for the post-season and won the team's first Stanley Cup since 1955.

### LOS ANGELES KINGS
1981-82 (-36)

Led by the "Triple Crown Line" of Marcel Dionne–Charlie Simmer–Dave Taylor, the Kings scored 337 goals in 1980–81 and finished with 99 points, the fourth best total in the league. Late in the season, Simmer broke his leg and took more than a year to recover in full. Consequently, the L.A. offense was less effective in 1981–82 and the team dropped to 63 points.

### CHICAGO BLACKHAWKS
1983-84 (-36)

The Hawks were a top club in 1982–83 with 104 points, only two behind the first place Edmonton Oilers. They were led by the forward line of Denis Savard-Steve Larmer-Al Secord along with defenseman Doug Wilson. Chicago was humiliated and outscored 26–11 by Edmonton in the semi-finals causing head coach Orval Tessier to recommend heart transplants for his team. The Hawks were still reeling the next year and dropped to 68 points.

### NEW YORK RANGERS
1984-85 (-31)

In 1983–84, the Rangers finished with 93 points but still only finished fourth in the strong Patrick Division. Undaunted by a match-up with the defending Cup-champion Islanders, they extended their crosstown rivals to a deciding fifth game in the preliminary round of the playoffs before losing in overtime. The team slipped to 62 points the next year but still finished fourth before they were swept by the Philadelphia Flyers again in the first round.

**1**

## MARCH 9, 1895
Queen's University 1    Montreal AAA 5

Although the Montreal Victorias had won the AHA (Amateur Hockey Association) title, they were not awarded the Stanley Cup, as they had expected. Instead, John Sweetland and Philip Ross, the Cup trustees, deemed that the previous year's winners, the Montreal AAA, should accept the challenge from Queen's. In a further twist, if Montreal AAA won, then the Vics would win the Cup, and if Queen's won, it would be awarded the bowl.

**2**

## DECEMBER 30, 1896
Montreal Vics 6    Winnipeg Vics 5

The Montreal Vics won the AHA title again, in February of 1896, and immediately accepted a challenge from the Winnipeg team of the same nickname. However, no good sheet of ice could be found, so the match had to wait until the start of the following winter. In the game, Montreal came from 4–2 down to win, and Ernie McLea recorded the first Stanley Cup hat trick when he scored the winner with just seconds left to play.

**3**

## DECEMBER 27, 1897
Montreal Vics 15    Ottawa Capitals 2

The Vics won the AHA championship for the third straight year and gladly accepted a chance to play the Caps, winners of the Central Canada Hockey Association honours. Although this was planned as a three-game series, Sweetland and Ross abandoned the idea after the first game because the teams were badly mismatched.

**4**

### FEBRUARY 15, 1899
Montreal Victorias 2     Winnipeg Victorias 1

### FEBRUARY 18, 1899
Montreal Victorias 3     Winnipeg Victorias 2

In two straight one-goal games, the Montreal Vics retained their Cup title before large crowds in Montreal. After a controversial penalty call against Winnipeg during the second game, the team left the ice. The referee himself then left and failed to appear for an hour, at which time he gave the Winnipegs five minutes to resume play. They didn't appear, and he awarded the game to Montreal.

**5**

### MARCH 14, 1899
Montreal Shamrocks 6    Queen's University 2

Formerly known as the Crystals, the Shamrocks made their first successful defense of the Cup thanks to Harry Trihey's hat trick. They had won the right to be challenged because they finished atop the standing of the CAHL (Canadian Amateur Hockey League).

**6**

### FEBRUARY 12, 1900
Montreal Shamrocks 4    Winnipeg Victorias 3

### FEBRUARY 14, 1900
Winnipeg Victorias 3    Montreal Shamrocks 2

### FEBRUARY 16, 1900
Montreal Shamrocks 5     Winnipeg Victorias 4

Played during the various league seasons, this was the closest of all challenges to date. Harry Trihey was again the star for the Montrealers, scoring three goals in the final game and seven overall as the Shamrocks won the series by the narrowest of margins.

**7**

### MARCH 5, 1900
Montreal Shamrocks 10   Halifax Crescents 2

### MARCH 7, 1900
Montreal Shamrocks 11   Halifax Crescents 0

Champions of the Maritime Hockey League, the Crescents won the right to challenge Montreal for the Cup, a challenge that was soundly defeated. Arthur Farrell set a new record by scoring four goals in a game, a feat he accomplished in both games of this series.

**8**

**JANUARY 29, 1901**

Winnipeg Victorias 4    Montreal Shamrocks 3

**JANUARY 31, 1901**

Winnipeg Victorias 2    Montreal Shamrocks 1 (OT)

The Cup was decided for the first time in overtime and the Winnipegs won the Cup for the first time since 1896. Dan Bain was the hero four minutes into the OT, and he played the games with a special mask to protect his injured face.

**9**

**JANUARY 21, 1902**

Toronto Wellingtons 3    Winnipeg Victorias 5

**JANUARY 23, 1902**

Toronto Wellingtons 3    Winnipeg Victorias 5

In a best-of-three challenge, the Wellingtons proved a good match for the Vics but wound up on the losing end in two consecutive games.

**10**

**MARCH 13, 1902**

Winnipeg Victorias 1    Montreal AAA 0

**MARCH 15, 1902**

Montreal AAA 5    Winnipeg Victorias 0

**MARCH 17, 1902**

Montreal AAA 2    Winnipeg Victorias 1

Winners of the first Stanley Cup in 1893, the AAA came back from defeat in game one to win the best-of-three 2–1. They trailed going into the third period of that deciding game, but two quick goals and a fierce defense gave them victory and took the Cup from the Toronto Wellingtons which had won the trophy less than two months previous.

# Most **CONSECUTIVE** Years
# **MISSING** the **PLAYOFFS**
(transferred teams not included)

---

### WASHINGTON CAPITALS    1974-82
EIGHT YEARS

These Caps were, without dispute, the worst team of all time. They joined the NHL in 1974, but did not take part in a playoff game until 1983. In their first season, they won one game of 40 on the road and eight overall, and surrendered 446 goals in 80 games. The next season was only marginally better, and it wasn't until '82–'83 that they had a .500 record.

### BOSTON BRUINS    1959-67
EIGHT YEARS

After winning the Cup in 1941, the Bruins had many fine teams for the next 15 years with the Kraut Line of Schmidt–Dumart–Bauer. But in the years leading up to the arrival of Bobby Orr, Boston was the worst in the league, winning just 62 games during one four-year stretch and giving fans even more reason to anticipate Orr's arrival with baited breath.

The Washington Capitals failed to make the playoffs in each their first eight NHL seaso

## DETROIT RED WINGS    1971-77
### SEVEN YEARS

Detroit went from Cup contender to gawdawful in a hurry. Backed
by Roger Crozier's Conn Smythe performance in the 1966 finals, it
seemed the Wings had championship results in the offing. But
Crozier's play became erratic, and the Wings missed the playoffs the
next three years. After a brief appearance in 1970, when they were
swept by Chicago in the first round, they then missed the playoffs for
the next seven seasons. In all, they missed out ten of eleven years.

## PITTSBURGH PENGUINS    1982-88
### SIX YEARS

It was because Pittsburgh was so bad that they were able to draft
Mario Lemieux, and it was because of Lemieux the Pens were able to
slip out of this long streak of playoff non-qualifying. Lemieux joined
Pittsburgh as an 18-year-old in 1984, but it was still four years before
he almost single-handedly put the team in the playoffs. After a brief
run in 1988, they were out again in '89 and then won the Cup the
next two years.

## NEW YORK ISLANDERS    1994-2000
### SIX YEARS

Few teams have gone from dynasty to ignominy as quickly and as
thoroughly as the Long Islanders. Once the class of the league, they
have missed the playoffs nine of the last 12 years, including the last
six straight. Crowds are down to about 7,000, management has
traded many of the fine young players, and the Coliseum is in ruin.
Yet in the early 1980s, no one could beat this team that won four
straight Cups from 1980 to 1983.

## CHICAGO BLACKHAWKS    1946-52
### SIX YEARS

The Blackhawks had one of the worst records in pro sports for 15
years or more. Between 1943 and 1958, they made the playoffs only
twice, and between 1935 and 1958 they won more than ten road
games only once. It wasn't until Jim Norris established a scouting
department that the Chicagos were able to build and develop talent,
and this in turn created a winning team that took the Stanley Cup
from Montreal in the spring of 1961.

# Eight Most **LOPSIDED** NHL
# **PLAYOFF GAMES**

(minimum 10 goals scored)

**1**
### MONTREAL 11    TORONTO 0
March 30, 1944

This was the fifth and last game of the best-of-seven semi-finals in a
series in which the Leafs scored only six goals. Montreal went on
to win the Cup by sweeping Chicago in a four-game finals.

**2**
### MONTREAL 10    TORONTO 3
March 29, 1945

This was the fourth game of the semi-finals and a complete aberration
from the rest of the series. Going into the game, the Leafs held a
commanding 3–1 lead and seemed destined to win, but Montreal
stayed alive with this hammering. Coach Happy Day and his team
recovered quickly, though, and the Leafs eliminated the Habs in the
next game with a closer 3–2 win.

**3**
### BOSTON 10    TORONTO 0
April 2, 1969

After winning four Stanley Cups in the first seven years of the
1960s, Punch Imlach's Leafs went into steep decline after
expansion and the team was victim to an offensive pounding from
Bobby Orr and his emerging Bruins. In fact, the Bruins won the
next game 7–0 and went on to eliminate the Leafs in four straight,
the last games for Imlach as coach of Toronto.

**4**
### BOSTON 10    ST. LOUIS 2
April 20, 1972

Orr and the Bruins were at it again in the second game of their semi-
finals with the Blues. They went on to win in four straight games and
then beat the Rangers in the finals to win their second Stanley Cup
in three years.

**5**

## RANGERS 10    LOS ANGELES 3
April 11, 1981

In the best-of-five preliminary round, the Rangers were definite underdogs. During the season, they were six games under .500 while the Kings finished with 99 points in the Norris Division. The Rangers took a 2–1 lead with this win, and then eliminated L.A. the next game.

**6**

## EDMONTON 10    CALGARY 2
April 17, 1983

Calgary took one of a series of poundings in this quarter-finals series against Gretzky's emerging dynasty. The Oilers scored 35 goals in the five games en route to a Stanley Cup showdown but couldn't continue their offensive ways in that series, losing to the Islanders in four straight.

**7**

## EDMONTON 11    CHICAGO 2
May 4, 1985

In the first game of the semi-finals, the Oilers established hemselves as the offensive champions they were. In the six games of the series, they scored an incredible 44 goals in eliminating an inferior Blackhawks team that could not keep up with the great Gretzky, Messier, Kurri, et al.

**8**

## LOS ANGELES 12    CALGARY 4
April 10, 1990

The year after winning the Stanley Cup, the Flames began a downward spiral that has yet to see them win a playoff series for the rest of the century. In this first-round matchup, they were hammered by the Kings, which now featured Gretzky who had been traded from the dreaded Oilers two years previous. The Kings went on from this game four shellacking to win the series in six.

# Six **FASTEST TRIPS** to the Stanley Cup Finals by an **EXPANSION TEAM**

**1**

### ST. LOUIS BLUES, YEAR 1

During the first year of expansion, one of the new clubs was ensured a spot in the final as Western Division playoff champions. St. Louis finished third in the regular season standings but, aided by ageing stars Doug Harvey, Dickie Moore, and Glenn Hall, the team managed to vanquish Philadelphia and Minnesota in consecutive seven-game series. In the finals they stayed close to Montreal but lost all four games by a single goal. Hall's brilliance in a losing cause earned him the Conn Smythe trophy.

Dickie Moore (with the puck) and Glenn Hall (in goal) helped the St. Louis Blues reach the Stanley Cup finals during their inaugural season in 1967-68.

## 2    FLORIDA PANTHERS, YEAR 3

The Panthers were a fast-skating and inspired crew during the 1995–96 season. Backstopped by veteran goalie John Vanbiesbrouck, they eliminated Boston in the opening round and then upset Philadelphia and Pittsburgh in the ensuing rounds. The upstart south Floridians met the powerful Colorado Avalanche in the final. Three of the four games were close, especially the Cup-clincher which lasted until Uwe Krupp's heroics in the third overtime period.

## 3    EDMONTON OILERS, YEAR 4

The Edmonton Oilers were an NHL powerhouse by 1981–82 but were upset by Los Angeles in the first round. The following year they were focused from the beginning and dropped only one match on the way to a showdown with the defending champion New York Islanders. In the finals, the experienced Islanders shut down Gretzky, Kurri, Messier, Coffey, and Anderson to win in four straight games. The setback proved to be full of valuable lessons that came in handy the next year when the Oilers went all the way.

## 4    BUFFALO SABRES, YEAR 5

Led by the "French Connection" line of Gilbert Perreault, Rick Martin, and René Robert, the 1974–75 edition of the Sabres finished tied for the most points in the NHL. In the post-season they handled Chicago and Montreal to earn a meeting with the defending champion Philadelphia Flyers in the finals. The young Buffalo squad lost the first two games at the dreaded Spectrum before evening the series at home on Robert's overtime winner in the fog-shrouded Memorial Auditorium. The Flyers spoiled the party by playing like champions in winning the last two games of the series.

## PHILADELPHIA FLYERS, YEAR 7

**5**

Prior to the 1973–74 season, the Flyers re-acquired goalie Bernie Parent from Toronto. This move proved to be the most significant transaction in franchise history. That year Philadelphia registered 112 points before defeating Atlanta and the New York Rangers to earn a Stanley Cup final berth against the Boston Bruins. In addition to Conn Smythe trophy winner Bernie Parent, it was Bobby Clarke's fiery leadership and the intimidating antics of several of its players that kept the Bruins at bay in the 4–2 series win. The Flyers' victory made them the first expansion team to win the Stanley Cup.

## NEW YORK ISLANDERS, YEAR 8

**6**

After a rough first year, the Islanders were a model expansion club. They quickly became competitive after adding Denis Potvin, Clark Gillies, and Bryan Trottier through the draft. The team reached the semifinals in 1975, 1976, 1977, and 1979 before getting to the final in 1980. They were technically the underdogs in the match-up against Philadelphia but quickly seized home ice advantage after Potvin's overtime winner in game two at the Spectrum. They began their run of four straight championships when Bob Nystrom tipped in the winner in the extra period of the sixth game.

# Ten Biggest **MISMATCHES IN** a
# **FIRST-ROUND PLAYOFF** Series

### 1986 OILERS VS. CANUCKS
(60-point differential)

The defending Stanley Cup champion Oilers dominated the league with a 119-point season while Vancouver barely qualified for the post-season with 59 points. The result of the series was predictable – the Oilers won in three straight games and outscored their opponents 17–5.

### 1996 RED WINGS VS. JETS
(53-point differential)

The Red Wings set an NHL record with 62 wins and piled up a remarkable 131 points while the Jets put up a respectable 78-point total. In their NHL swan song, the Manitobans competed well in extending the favourites to six games before relocating to Phoenix.

### 1985 FLYERS VS. RANGERS
(51-point differential)

The Flyers recorded an excellent 113-point season while the Rangers qualified for the playoffs with just 62 points. The underdogs made a game of it as two games were decided by a goal but Philly still prevailed in three straight matches.

### 1982 OILERS VS. KINGS
(48-point differential)

The Oilers broke through as one of the league's dominant teams with 111 points while the Kings declined to 63 points without the "Triple Crown Line." In one of the biggest upsets in playoff history, the underdogs from California stunned the cocky Oilers three games to two in a high-scoring battle.

## 5 1980 FLYERS VS. OILERS
(47-point differential)

The young Oilers managed 69 points in their first NHL season but the Flyers set an NHL record by going undefeated in 35 straight games on the way to recording 116 points. Led by Wayne Gretzky, the underdogs put up a good fight by sending two games into overtime but were still swept by the more experienced Flyers.

## 6 1978 FLYERS VS. ROCKIES
(46-point differential)

The Flyers cruised to a 105-point season while the Rockies qualified for the playoffs for the first time in franchise history despite the fact they only won 19 games and accumulated a mere 59 points. The upstarts were swept in two games in the best-of-three preliminary round but lost in overtime in game one and 3–1 in game two.

## 7 1984 OILERS VS. JETS
(46-point differential)

After being swept by the Islanders in the 1983 finals, the Oilers were focused throughout the 1983–84 regular season. They accumulated a league-high 119 points while the Jets had a mediocre 73-point year. The eventual Cup champions swept Winnipeg in four games and outscored them 18–7.

## 8 1977 BLACKHAWKS VS. ISLANDERS
(43-point differential)

The Islanders were an established regular season force with 106 points while the Hawks were in decline with 63 points. The favourites swept the two-game series with little difficulty on their way to a third straight appearance in the semi-finals.

## 9

### 1982 ISLANDERS VS. PENGUINS
(43-point differential)

The reigning Stanley Cup champion Islanders registered 118 points and were expected to roll over their lesser opponents who amassed 75 points. In one of the tightest series that year, the Penguins extended the champs to overtime in the fifth and deciding game before John Tonelli ended their dreams of an upset.

## 10

### 1989 FLAMES VS. CANUCKS
(43-point differential)

The Flames' 117 points led the NHL for the second straight season while the Canucks had a decent if unspectacular 74-point year. Vancouver gave the eventual Cup champions all they could handle in the seven-game series. In the deciding match, Jim Peplinski scored the winner moments after Mike Vernon stopped the Canucks' Stan Smyl on a breakaway.

### **1** FRANK BOUCHER
April 7, 1928

A centre, Boucher scored the extra period winner in the second
game of the finals against the Montreal Maroons. This was the
same contest that saw coach Lester Patrick don the pads as an
emergency replacement for injured starter Lorne Chabot. The
Rangers went on to win their first Stanley Cup three games to two.

### **2** BUTCH KEELING
March 21, 1929

Keeling was a solid scorer from the left-wing during twelve seasons
spent mostly with the Rangers. He scored the only goal of the
quarter-final series against the arch-rival New York Americans to
propel the "Blueshirts" into the semi-finals against Toronto.

### **3** FRANK BOUCHER
March 26, 1929

The centre on the "Bread Line" fired the overtime winner against
the Toronto Maple Leafs in the second game semi-finals. The
Rangers swept the two-game series and moved on to face the
Boston Bruins in the first NHL final involving two American teams.

### **4** BUN COOK
March 26, 1932

Cook's overtime heroics evened the semi-final series with the
Montreal Canadiens at one game. The Habs won the opener but
Cook's goal reversed the momentum in the series and sent New Yor
on to a three games to one win.

### **5** BILL COOK
April 13, 1933

One of the top Rangers of all time, Cook scored the NHL's first
Cup-clinching goal in overtime against the Toronto Maple Leafs.
New York claimed the series three games to one to win their
second Stanley Cup.

Centre Frank Boucher scored the New York Rangers' first playoff overtime goal on April 7, 1928.

## 6 BABE PRATT
March 25, 1937

A gifted offensive defenseman, Pratt eliminated the Maple Leafs in the second game of the quarter-finals. That year, the Rangers extended the Detroit Red Wings to the maximum five games in a hotly-contested final.

## 7 CLINT SMITH
March 30, 1939

The Rangers bowed out in the semi-finals against the Boston Bruins. The Bruins led the series 3–0 but the Rangers eventually forced a seventh game. Smith's overtime goal in game five kept the Rangers alive.

## 8 ALF PIKE
April 2, 1940

During his rookie season utility forward Alf Pike helped the Rangers win their fourth Stanley Cup. In the final against Toronto he scored the first of the team's three overtime winners in the series to stake the "Blueshirts" to a 1–0 series lead.

## 9 MUZZ PATRICK
April 11, 1940

The son of Lester Patrick provided the extra period heroics at Maple Leaf Gardens which gave New York a 3–2 series lead in the finals. He and brother Lynn kept the family tradition going strong by playing key roles in the Rangers' Cup triumph.

## 10 BRYAN HEXTALL, SR.
April 13, 1940

One of the top players of his era, Hextall started a family ritual of h own by making the NHL. He scored the Cup-clincher in overtime against Turk Broda and later saw his sons Bryan and Dennis as we as grandson Ron excel in the big leagues.

# Most HALL OF FAMERS on a
# STANLEY CUP TEAM

## 11   MONTREAL CANADIENS: 1972-73

Ken Dryden, Guy Lapointe, Serge Savard,
Larry Robinson, Jacques Laperrière, Yvan
Cournoyer, Frank Mahovlich, Jacques Lemaire,
Henri Richard, Guy Lafleur, Steve Shutt

This powerful Habs team had little trouble winning the Cup. They
beat Buffalo in six games in the quarter-finals, then eliminated
Philadelphia in five, and won the Cup convincingly in six games
over Chicago. Many of these players were to remain with the team
during part of their four-Cup run later in the '70s.

## 10   MONTREAL CANADIENS: 1955-56

Jacques Plante, Doug Harvey, Butch Bouchard,
Tom Johnson, Jean Béliveau, Bernie Geoffrion,
Bert Olmstead, Maurice Richard, Dickie Moore,
Henri Richard

This was the first of five consecutive Stanley Cups, but it was this
team that had the most Hall of Famers on it. With future teams,
coach Toe Blake always made sure to insert two or three rookies into
the lineup to keep the team sharp and young, but a core of the older
players were with the team for all five wins.

## 10   TORONTO MAPLE LEAFS: 1961-62

Johnny Bower, Tim Horton, Allan Stanley, Al
Arbour, Red Kelly, George Armstrong, Frank
Mahovlich, Bert Olmstead, Bob Pulford, Dave Keon

This was the first Cup for the Leafs under coach Punch Imlach after
coming close in '59 and '60 before losing to Montreal in the finals.
This year, they beat the Rangers and then Chicago in six games each
to win the Cup, the series-winning game a 2–1 score in Chicago.

## 10 TORONTO MAPLE LEAFS: 1963-64

Johnny Bower, Tim Horton, Allan Stanley, Andy Bathgate, Al Arbour, Red Kelly, George Armstrong, Dave Keon, Bob Pulford, Frank Mahovlich

Imlach kept his winning team virtually intact for the three years of the team's dynastic Cup run, and this was the historic year the Leafs won two straight seven-game series, first against Montreal in the semis and then Detroit in the finals.

## 10 TORONTO MAPLE LEAFS: 1966-67

Johnny Bower, Terry Sawchuk, Marcel Pronovost, Tim Horton, Allan Stanley, Red Kelly, George Armstrong, Dave Keon, Bob Pulford, Frank Mahovlich

Incredibly, Imlach won this Cup with the oldest lineup in league history. By this time, Bower, Sawchuk, Stanley, Kelly, Armstrong, and Pronovost were all either close to or over 40. It was the last year of the Original Six, the last time Montreal and Toronto played in the finals, and the last time the Leafs won the Cup.

# FEWEST Hall of FAMERS on a Stanley CUP TEAM

### 1     CHICAGO BLACKHAWKS: 1937-38
Earl Seibert

In this the greatest anomaly, a Cup-winning team without great players on it won the 1938 trophy as the Hawks defeated the Leafs 3–1 in the best-of-five finals. It was also the year that the Hawks had some eight American players in their lineup as a stunt by team owner Major Frederick McLaughlin.

### 3     SEATTLE METROPOLITANS: 1916-17
Hap Holmes, Frank Foyston, Jack Walker

The last pre-NHL team to win the Cup and the first from the United States, the Mets won this best-of-five in four games. After losing the first to the Canadiens 8–4, the Seattles got stronger and stronger, winning game two 6–1, then 4–1, and finally 9–1.

Earl Seibert was the only member of the Chicago Blackhawks' 1938 Stanley Cup team to be inducted into the Hockey Hall of Fame.

### 3   CHICAGO BLACKHAWKS: 1933-34
Lionel Conacher, Art Coulter, Charlie Gardiner

Mush March scored the Cup-winner in overtime of game four, and the Hawks beat Detroit 1–0 in that deciding game. The star of the series was goalie Gardiner who played in every game for Chicago for six straight seasons and who had 42 shutouts in just 316 career regular season games.

### 3   TORONTO MAPLE LEAFS: 1944-45
Ted Kennedy, Babe Pratt, Sweeney Schriner

Someone had to win the Cup during the war years, and the badly depleted Leafs' line-up won without goalie Turk Broda who was replaced by "Ulcers" McCool. Kennedy led the playoffs in scoring as a teenager, and Pratt scored the winning goal in his last full NHL season as the Leafs beat the Red Wings in seven games.

### 3   PHILADELPHIA FLYERS: 1973-74
Bill Barber, Bobby Clarke, Bernie Parent

The Broad Street Bullies lost to Montreal the previous finals, but this year, with a lineup equally thin on talent and replete with goonery, beat Bobby Orr and the Boston Bruins in six games to make them the first expansion team to win the Cup. Of course, key to the victory was the sensational goaltending of Parent, without whom the team would never have won.

### 3   PHILADELPHIA FLYERS: 1974-75
Bill Barber, Bobby Clarke, Bernie Parent

Again it was the play of Conn Smythe Trophy winner Parent that beat the surprise finalist Buffalo Sabres in six games. Although he allowed nine goals in games three and four, he gave up only three goals in the other four games and the Flyers defeated Punch Imlach' emerging team which, unfortunately, peaked with this playoffs.

# FIRST and LAST GOALS in
## Original Six BUILDINGS

### MAPLE LEAF GARDENS, TORONTO

**FIRST**   Mush March (Chicago), November 12, 1931

**LAST**   Bob Probert (Chicago), February 13, 1999

### MONTREAL FORUM

**FIRST**   Billy Boucher (Canadiens), November 29, 1924 vs. Toronto

**LAST**   Andrei Kovalenko (Canadiens), March 11, 1996  vs. Dallas

### DETROIT OLYMPIA

**FIRST**   Johnny Sheppard (Detroit), November 22, 1927 vs. Ottawa

**LAST**   Garry Unger (St. Louis), October 11, 1978

### BOSTON GARDEN

**FIRST**   Sylvio Mantha (Canadiens), November 20, 1928

**LAST**   Adam Oates (Boston), May 14, 1995 vs. New Jersey

### CHICAGO STADIUM

**FIRST**   Vic Ripley (Chicago), December 15, 1929 vs. Pittsburgh Pirates

**LAST**   Mike Gartner (Toronto), April 28, 1994

### MADISON SQUARE GARDEN, NEW YORK

**FIRST**   Shorty Green (New York Americans), December 15, 1925 vs. Canadiens

**LAST**   Jean Ratelle (Rangers), February 11, 1968 vs. Detroit

### 1 HENRI RICHARD, 1936

The only Hall of Famer of the group, the "Pocket Rocket" joined his older brother Maurice in 1955 and began a distinguished career that in many ways resembled the Rocket's. Henri played his entire 20-year career with the Habs, but unlike Maurice he was able to earn more than 1,000 points before retiring. He won an extraordinary eleven Stanley Cups, played in ten All-Star Gamess, and was duly elected into the Hockey Hall of Fame the minute he became eligible.

### 2 KARI ELORANTA, 1956

One of the first wave of Finnish players to join the NHL in the early 1980s, Eloranta played only three full years in North America during a career that was mostly international in scope. He played for Finland at every level of IIHF competition, notably the World Juniors, Worlds, and Olympics, but also played in the Swedish Elite League for a number of years. His three Olympic appearances came in 1980, '88, and '92, and he also played in the 1991 Canada Cup.

### 3 DAN DAOUST, 1960

One of the more popular Toronto Maple Leafs because of his tenacity as a defensive centreman, Daoust played most of the '80s in the Blue and White. He was never drafted but was signed as a free agent with the Canadiens before coming to Toronto in 1982 for a 3rd-round draft choice. After being let go by the Leafs, Daoust pursued hockey in Europe, playing a number of years in the comfortable but skilled Swiss League.

## JIM DOBSON, 1960

The most obscure player of this Leap Year list, Dobson played just 12 NHL games over a sporadic four-year career that was punctuated by long stops in the minors. Drafted by Minnesota in 1979, he played just eight games with the North Stars before being traded to the lowly Colorado Rockies. In Denver, he played just three games and then signed as a free agent with the Nordiques. After just one game, he spent the rest of his years in the minors, never having recorded a single NHL point.

The "Pocket Rocket," Henri Richard, moves in on Eddie Giacomin with Jean Ratelle close behind.

## LYNDON BYERS, 1964

Byers's 279-game career was stretched out over ten years, eight of those involving stints in both the NHL and minors. Resilient and determined, he played his way back to the NHL every time he was demoted. After nine years with Boston, he signed with San Jose for the '92–'93 season, but he dressed for only 18 games before being sent to the minors for good.

### 1 MINNESOTA FIGHTING SAINTS
1976–77

A solid franchise from 1972–75, the Saints folded midway through the '75–'76 season. At the same time, the Cleveland Crusaders were an equally successful team for a few years, but during the summer of 1976 the team had to move and the owners chose Minnesota as their new home, keeping the nickname Fighting Saints that had been previously used. This second incarnation of the team, however, suffered from awful attendance and non-existent season's ticket sales and folded after 42 games of the '76–'77 season.

### 2 DENVER SPURS
1975–76

The Spurs took their name from the Western League team of the same name and played in the new McNichols Arena. But they went winless in their first eight games at home and averaged around 3,000 fans a game. After just 41 games, the team moved to Ottawa and became the Civics.

### 3 OTTAWA CIVICS
1975–76

Ottawa became a vacant WHA city after the Nationals had left for Toronto to become the Toros. The Civics lasted exactly 15 days from start to finish. They won one of their seven games, and their most famous player was Ralph Backstrom. This was the first team to fold during the season that was neither replaced nor relocated.

### 4 MICHIGAN STAGS
1974–75

After two dismal seasons as the Los Angeles Sharks, the team move
in April 1974 to Detroit as the Michigan Stags as an alternative to t
then struggling Red Wings of the NHL. But the Stags were an awfu
team and crowds were around 2,000 at Cobo Hall. On January 18,
1975, the team folded.

### 5 BALTIMORE BLADES
1974–75

The aforementioned Stags were packed off to Baltimore to continue
the Michigan schedule out of the Baltimore Civic Centre. However,
the team continued to lose and the city hardly embraced their
spontaneously-arrived team, and at the end of the season the Blades
were no more.

### 6 NEW YORK GOLDEN BLADES
1973–74

The New York Raiders played in the WHA for one season, 1972–73
and the next summer changed their name to Golden Blades. The
team played out of Madison Square Garden, but crowds were tiny
and after fewer than two months the team relocated to New Jersey
where they were christened the Knights.

### 7 NEW JERSEY KNIGHTS
1973–74

Ergo, the Knights played out of a place called the Cherry Hill
Arena, but they were barely able to finish the season for lack of
finances, and even then before small crowds. The team had André
Lacroix in the lineup (he scored 111 points), but they finished in
last place and moved to San Diego to start the next season.

## 8 OTTAWA NATIONALS
1972-73

Coached by Billy Harris, the Nats played during the inaugural season of WHA hockey, 1972–73. However, the team was playing before groups of 3,000 people, and although they made it into the playoffs their financial situation was bleak. The Toronto Maple Leafs missed the 1973 playoffs, so the Nats transferred their home playoff games to the Gardens where they drew 5,000. As a result, the team moved to Toronto permanently to start the next season.

## 9 PHILADELPHIA BLAZERS
1972-73

Originally the Miami Screaming Eagles, the team eventually moved to Philly before having played a game. They became headliners immediately after signing both Bernie Parent and Derek Sanderson to contracts, but both were injured early in the season and the Blazers were awful without them. After one season, new owner Jim Pattison took the team to Vancouver.

**1**

### WAYNE CARLETON

Carleton scored 37 goals and 92 points after remaining
with the franchise following its move from Ottawa. In the playoffs,
he contributed 14 points in twelve games as the Toronto club
extended the Chicago Cougars to seven games before bowing out in
the semi-finals.

**2**

### WAYNE DILLON

A scoring star with the Toronto Marlboros in junior,
Dillon chose to stay in the city with the WHA's Toros. He scored 16(
points in two seasons and was considered one of the league's most
gentlemanly players.

**3**

### GILLES GRATTON

One of hockey's all-time eccentrics, Gratton was adept
at stopping the puck. He won 56 games in two seasons with the
Toros and took part in the 1974 Summit Series between the WHA
All-Stars and the Soviet national team.

**4**

### PAUL HENDERSON

Henderson stayed in Toronto but switched leagues prior
to the 1974–75 schedule. He took part in the WHA's 1974 Summit
Series versus the Soviet Union then scored 119 points in two seasor
with the Toros.

**5**

### PAT HICKEY

After a stellar junior career when he captained the
Hamilton Red Wings, Hickey's signing was a major coup for the
Toros. A speedster with a natural scoring touch, the left-winger
recorded 26- and 35-goal seasons in 1973–74 and 1974–75.

### 6 FRANK MAHOVLICH

The "Big M" returned to Toronto and played two seasons with the Toros. He began his WHA tenure by representing Canada in the 1974 Summit Series versus the USSR. He then scored 72 goals over two seasons with the Toros and remained with the franchise when it relocated to Birmingham in 1976.

### 7 MARK NAPIER

An explosive skater with natural offensive talent, Napier was a junior phenom with the Toronto Marlboros of the OHA. During the 1975–76 season, he registered 43 goals and 93 points for the Toros and was chosen the WHA's top rookie.

### 8 VACLAV NEDOMANSKY

The immensely talented Czech caused quite a stir when he signed with the Toros prior to the 1974–75 season. He didn't disappoint and recorded 41 and 56 goals during his two years in Toronto. Following the 1975–76 season he was named the WHA's most gentlemanly player.

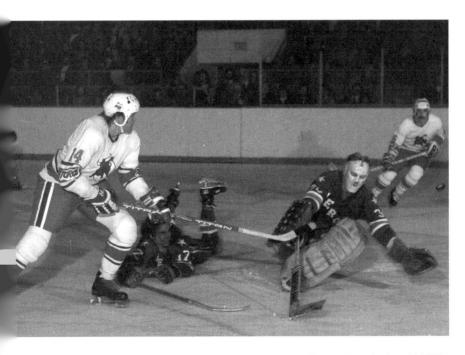

Vaclav Nedomansky scored 97 goals over two seasons for the Toronto Toros in the mid-1970s.

### 1   BILL ANDERSON

Anderson's one and only NHL game came in the 1942–43 playoffs for the Boston Bruins. A native of Tillsonburg, Ontario, he never played another pro game after this season.

### 2   HARRY BELL

Although he only played one game, Bell had an assist for the Rangers in 1946–47. He spent the rest of the year with the minor league team, the New York Rovers, and played a few more years with a variety of non-NHL clubs.

### 3   GORD BYERS

Byers, too, had an assist in his only game, for Boston in '49–'50. He had played junior with the Teepees in St. Catharines, and spent the rest of his career with numerous minor pro teams of varying quality.

### 4   DON CHERRY

Famous not only as a broadcaster but a player who was left to die in the minors 15 years in all, "Grapes" got into one NHL game, a playoff game with Boston, in 1955, against the Montreal Canadiens at the Forum.

### 5   NORM COLLINGS

Collings had an assist for the Montreal Canadiens during the 1934–35 season, one which saw the Habs finish with a sub-.500 record and lose to the Rangers in the first round of the playoffs. He played two more years in the minors before retiring.

### 6   BUCK DAVIES

His only NHL game came during the 1948 playoffs for the New York Rangers against the Detroit Red Wings. A slight 5'6" and 162 pounds, he played 13 more seasons of pro hockey in the AHL and EHL, but never again in the NHL.

### GORD HAIDY

**7**

In a 20-year professional career, Haidy's one flash of NHL glory occurred during the 1950 playoffs with the Red Wings during which the team went on to win the Cup.

### ROLLY HUARD

**8**

Huard's ratio success is unparalleled in NHL history. Although he played only one game, he scored a goal in that game during the 1931–32 season with the Maple Leafs, one of only two players to have accomplished this rare feat (Dean Morton is the other). Despite his heroics, he was demoted to Syracuse the day after his heroic NHL entry and never saw the big top again.

### JIM JAMIESON

**9**

In his one game with the Rangers he was a minor hit, recording an assist during the 1943–44 season. Otherwise, he spent his decade in hockey in leagues far removed from the NHL.

### TIM McBURNEY

**10**

Another player who recorded an assist in his only game, McBurney played for Chicago during the '52–'53 season before spending six years with the Soo in the Northern Ontario league where he was an outstanding scorer.

# Eight Players Who Hold **SINGLE-SEASON RECORDS** for **MORE** Than **ONE FRANCHISE**

### WAYNE GRETZKY
Most assists in a season — Edmonton/L.A.

When Gretzky set the NHL single-season point record of 215 with Edmonton in 1985–86, he established a club record with 163 assists. In 1990–91, he set up 122 goals to establish a new standard for the Los Angeles Kings.

### WAYNE GRETZKY
Most points in a season — Edmonton/L.A.

The "Great One" set the Edmonton and NHL record with 215 point in 1985–86. Following the emotional trade to Los Angeles, he surpassed Kings' legend Marcel Dionne with 168 points during his first season in southern California.

### GLENN HALL
Most shutouts in a season — Detroit/St. Louis

Although best remembered as the star netminder on the Chicago Blackhawks, Hall carved a place in history with the Red Wings and Blues. In 1955–56, he equalled Sawchuk's year-old record of twelve shutouts. During the 1968–69 season, he set the St. Louis Blues' record with eight blank sheets while sharing the goaltending duties with Jacques Plante.

### LARRY MURPHY
Most points by a defenseman in a season — L.A./Washington

During a stellar rookie season in 1980–81, Murphy set a new record for Kings' defensemen with 76 points. Many of his assists came while working the power play with the "Triple Crown Line" of Dionne, Simmer, and Taylor. Six years later, he established a new mark for Washington rearguards with 81 points.

## PAUL COFFEY

Most points by a defenseman in a season — Edmonton/Pittsburgh

One of the most exciting offensive blueliners in league history, Coffey often stood out even though he was surrounded by superstars in Edmonton. In 1985–86, his 138 points set a new Oilers' record for defensemen and came within one of tying Bobby Orr's NHL standard. Coffey later set the record for a Pittsburgh defensemen with 113 points in 1988–89.

Paul Coffey set the record for the most points by a defenseman in a season for both Edmonton and Pittsburgh.

### 6 TEEMU SELANNE
Most points in a season — Winnipeg (Phoenix)/Anaheim

While shattering the rookie scoring record with 76 goals and 132 points in 1992–93, Selanne set franchise marks as well. After a trade brought him to Anaheim, he formed a lethal partnership with Paul Kariya and set the Mighty Ducks' record with 109 points.

### 7 PHIL HOUSLEY
Most points by a defenseman in a season — Buffalo/Winnipeg (Phoenix)

The slick playmaker from Minnesota set the Sabres record with 81 points in 1989–90. He was sent to Winnipeg in the Dale Hawerchuk trade and scored a franchise record 79 points in '92–'93.

### 8 TIE DOMI
Most penalty minutes in a season — Winnipeg (Phoenix)/Toronto

A hard-working enforcer and popular leader in the dressing-room, Domi registered 347 penalty minutes for the Winnipeg Jets in 1993–94. In 1997–98, he broke Tiger Williams' Maple Leafs record with 365 minutes served.

# Ten **RECORDS** Wayne **GRETZKY** **NEVER** Broke

**1** **MOST POINTS IN ONE GAME**
10 — Darryl Sittler

Twice Gretzky got eight points, the closest he came to Sittler's hallowed record. On November 19, 1983, Gretzky had three goals and five assists against New Jersey. It was after this game that he called the Devils a Mickey Mouse organization. On January 4, 1984, against the Minnesota North Stars, the Great One scored four goals and four assists.

 **2** **MOST SEASONS**
26 — Gordie Howe

One of the first comments Gretzky made after announcing his retirement was that Gordie's record was intact. Gretzky played 20 seasons, well short of Mr. Hockey's mark for longevity.

**3** **MOST GAMES**
1,767 — Gordie Howe

Again, Gretzky played 1,487 games, some 300 shy of Howe's mark. But in a career filled with international tournaments and extended playoffs that Howe never competed in, that gap is actually much smaller (though, of course, Howe's regular season was also shorter).

 **4** **MOST GOALS ONE GAME**
7 — Joe Malone

Gretzky scored five goals in a game on four occasions but, like Sittler's ten points, never came close to the record.

**5** **MOST ASSISTS, ONE PERIOD**
5 — Dale Hawerchuk

Three times did Gretzky have seven assists in a game, but never more than three in any one period.

Wayne Gretzky removes his skates after playing his last NHL game for the New York Range

## 6   MOST POINTS, ONE PERIOD

6 — Bryan Trottier

Gretzky had four points in a period on a number of occasions, but Trottier's remarkable flurry against the Rangers on December 23, 1978, remains the standard for a period just as Sittler's is for a game.

## 7   MOST REGULAR SEASON O/T GOALS, CAREER

11 — Steve Thomas

Although he had 15 career overtime assists, Gretzky had just two goals in regular season overtime.

## 8   MOST 30+ GOAL SEASONS

17 — Mike Gartner

Gretzky's streak stopped at 13 in 1992–93 when he missed the first half of the season with a serious back injury. He wound up playing just 45 games for Los Angeles, finishing with 16 goals.

## 9   CONSECUTIVE GOAL-SCORING STREAK

16 — Harry Broadbent

Between December 9–30, 1981, Gretzky scored in nine straight games, the longest continuous scoring streak of his career but well short of Broadbent's league record.

## 10   ANY TIME RECORD

(i.e., fastest goal from start of game, period, etc.)

Despite owning or sharing some 60-odd NHL records, Gretzky's forte was never fast goals from the start of a period or game, or multi-goals in a very short period of time.

**1**

### WAYNE GRETZKY
Career totals: 894 goals 1,963 assists 2,857 points

Though not impossible, it is highly unlikely that any player will ever play twenty outstanding NHL seasons similar to Wayne Gretzky. The "Great One" launched an all-out assault on the NHL record book and set a host of standards that will remain for generations.

**2**

### GLENN HALL
502 consecutive games by a goaltender

Between the start of the 1955–56 season and the first twelve games of the 1962–63 schedule, Hall played every game for the Detroit Red Wings and then Chicago Blackhawks. This remarkable achievement spoke volumes for his durability and continued excellence. In 1960–61, Hall led Chicago to its first Stanley Cup since 1938.

**3**

### TERRY SAWCHUK
103 regular season shutouts

Considered by many to be the greatest netminder in the history of the game, Sawchuk led the NHL in shutouts four times. He led the Detroit Red Wings to three Stanley Cups and combined with Johnny Bower to bring championship glory to Toronto in 1967. Since expansion, the closest anyone has come to his career shutout total was Tony Esposito who finished with 76.

**4**

### WAYNE GRETZKY
215 points 1984–85

Despite playing 14 more seasons, not even the "Great One" himself could exceed this astonishing single-season output. The closest any player came to even topping 200 points was Mario Lemieux's 199 points in 1988–89. It was an overwhelming year even for Gretzky, and he capped it off by leading the Oilers to their second straight Stanley Cup.

## PHIL ESPOSITO

550 shots on goal 1970-71

For years "Espo" parked himself in front of the opposition net and used his strength and patented quick release to beat goaltenders. The explosive offense of the Bruins in 1970–71 was generated by Bobby Orr's spectacular rushes and Esposito's determination in the slot. The second highest single season shots on goal total was Paul Kariya's 429 in 1998–99.

## HENRI RICHARD

11 Stanley Cups as a player

"The Pocket Rocket" was a tremendous player who was also in the right place in the right time. His Hall of Fame credentials were unquestionable. His career was also timely as he earned a place in the Habs' line-up in time to be a part of the team's five straight Stanley Cups in the 1950s. Richard later won four Stanley Cups between 1965 and 1969 along with two in the 1970s before retiring in 1975.

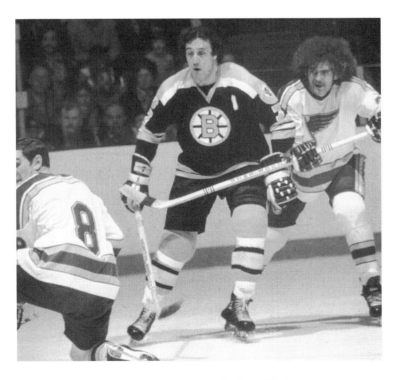

Boston sniper Phil Esposito fired 550 shots at enemy goalies during the 1970–71 season.

**7** ## GORDIE HOWE
26 NHL seasons

One of the icons of the game, Howe played a physical style that
saw him nearly killed once and badly hurt on a number of other
occasions. He was a brilliant right-winger who helped Detroit win
four Stanley Cups. Howe's physical condition allowed him to play
25 seasons in the league, ending in 1970–71. He returned at the age
of 52 for one last hurrah when the Hartford Whalers joined the
NHL in 1979–80.

**8** ## DARRYL SITTLER
10 points in a game February 7, 1976

The Toronto captain victimized the Boston Bruins for six goals and
four assists during an 11–4 romp at Maple Leaf Gardens. Not even
Gretzky or Lemieux could top this effort. It was an almost spooky
night as everything Sittler tried seemed to work. He finished his Hall
of Fame career with 1,121 points and a long standing place in the
NHL record book.

**9** ## MONTREAL CANADIENS
5 Consecutive Stanley Cups

Arguments will always rage concerning the greatest team of all
time. The Habs of the late 1950s were the only team to spend a half
decade at the top of the hockey world. The Islanders and Oilers
came close in the 1980s but, with player salaries and free agency,
the days of hockey dynasties seem to be over.

**10** ## PHILADELPHIA FLYERS
35-game unbeaten streak 1979–80

The Flyers were a solid mix of veterans, young players, and utility
workers in 1979–80. Between October 14, 1979, and January 6, 198
nobody could beat them. Philadelphia went 25–0–10 during the
streak and eventually reached the Stanley Cup final later that year.
In the process of setting this record, they bettered the old mark of 2
games without a loss set by the Montreal Canadiens in 1977–78.

# MOST Regular Season GAMES PLAYED, One Season

**1**
### JIMMY CARSON — 86

Traded by Detroit to Los Angeles midway through the 1992–93 season, Carson managed to extend the already long 84-game season by playing the full schedule plus two. He managed to score 37 combined goals and helped the Kings to their first-ever appearance in the Stanley Cup finals that spring.

**2**
### BOB KUDELSKI — 86

Like Carson, Kudelski was traded during the two years the NHL played 84 games. Kudelski was sent by Ottawa to Florida, a team that had played two fewer games. And, like Carson, the trade had only a positive effect on him as he scored 40 goals that season.

**3**
### GLENN ANDERSON — 85

Anderson was fortunate enough to be sent by a very talented Toronto team to an even better Rangers team at the trade deadline during the 1993–94 season. While the Leafs went to the semi-finals, the Blueshirts won their first Stanley Cup in more than fifty years.

**4**
### MARK LAMB — 85

Lamb, too, was traded near that 1994 deadline, by Ottawa to Philadelphia. However, the Flyers didn't make the playoffs and he scored just once in 19 games. Early the following season he was traded to Montreal and that signalled the beginning of the end of his career.

**5**
### JOE REEKIE — 85

Reekie was sent from Tampa to Washington at that same deadline, and in the final 12 games of the season he scored not a single goal with the Caps. However, he was a big, reliable defenseman who was still with the club during its improbable march to the 1998 finals.

135

### CRAIG JANNEY — 84

**6** Traded by San Jose to Winnipeg on March 18, 1996, Janney remained with the Jets/Coyotes franchise for two years before moving on to Tampa and Long Island. Although his scoring days are on their way out, he is still a reliable two-way centre.

### DARRYL SYDOR — 84

**7** Sydor was traded from the Kings to the Stars in Dallas in February 1996, and has been in the Lone Star State ever since. A talented offensive defenseman, he played two more than the regulation 82 games as a result of the trade and went on to win a Cup with Dallas in the spring of 1999.

### BRAD MARSH — 83

**8** One of the most durable defensive defensemen of the modern era, Marsh played 83 games during the 1981–82 season between Calgary and Philadelphia, scoring an incredible two goals in 66 games with the Flyers (his career best was three in one season). It was one of five times during his 15 years in the NHL that he played the full schedule.

# SEVEN Best Players DRAFTED from the Brandon WHEAT KINGS

**1**

### BRIAN PROPP

During his last season of junior, Propp scored 94 goals with extraordinary consistency while helping Brandon reach the Memorial Cup final. He was chosen 14th overall by the Philadelphia Flyers in 1979 and went on to become one of the most prolific scorers in the history of the franchise. Propp scored at least 40 goals on four occasions and helped the club reach three Stanley Cup finals. He later helped Boston and Minnesota reach the final round and then joined Hartford in 1993 for one final season. In all, he had 425 goals and 1,004 points in fifteen NHL seasons.

**2**

### GLENN HANLON

A popular and successful goalie wherever he went, Hanlon led the WCJHL in shutouts in each of his last two junior seasons. He played on a weak Vancouver team, moved on to St. Louis briefly, and then to the New York Rangers for parts of four seasons. He recorded a personal-high of 28 wins in 1983–84 but was eventually traded to Detroit where he helped the Wings reach the semi-finals in 1987 and 1988. He retired in 1991 with 167 wins and 13 shutouts.

Glenn Hanlon began his NHL career tending goal for the Vancouver Canucks.

## 3 BILL DERLAGO

An explosive scorer in junior, Derlago set a league record with 96 goals in 1976–77. He was drafted fourth overall by Vancouver in 1978 but spent the majority of his career with the Toronto Maple Leafs. Derlago scored at least 30 goals four times and registered a personal-best 84 points in 1981–82. He later played for Boston, Winnipeg, and Quebec before retiring in 1987 with 416 career points.

## 4 LAURIE BOSCHMAN

A junior linemate of Propp, Boschman was chosen ninth overall by Toronto in the 1979 Entry Draft. After a slow start with the Maple Leafs and later the Edmonton Oilers, his career blossomed when he was traded to the Winnipeg Jets in March 1983. Boschman became a solid two-way centre for the Jets and recorded four 20-goal seasons. He played briefly with New Jersey and Ottawa before retiring in 1993 with 577 career points in 1,009 games.

## 5 BRAD McCRIMMON

Another member of the Wheat Kings' 1979 powerhouse, McCrimmon was chosen 15th overall by the Boston Bruins later that summer. During his three years in Beantown his solid play was overshadowed by Ray Bourque. Prior to the 1982–83 season he was traded to Philadelphia where he became a key part of the team's run to the 1985 and 1987 Stanley Cup finals. In 1989 he contributed to the Calgary Flames' first Stanley Cup and later played with Detroit, Hartford, and Phoenix before retiring in 1997.

## 6 TREVOR KIDD

Kidd led the WCJHL with 125 appearances for the Wheat Kings in 1989–90. He was part of Team Canada's three straight gold medal wins at the World Junior championships from 1990 to 1992. Chosen 11th overall in the 1990 Entry Draft by the Calgary Flames he led all NHL goalies in games played in 1994–95 while recording personal high of 22 wins. Kidd spent a year in Carolina before a trade brought him to Florida in 1999–2000.

## WADE REDDEN

**7**

A complete package on defense, Redden starred on the Wheat Kings for three years and helped Canada win gold at the World Junior championships in 1995 and 1996. He was the second player chosen in the 1995 Entry Draft, by the New York Islanders, but ended up in Ottawa after a major trade in January 1996. Redden immediately became a workhorse on the improved Ottawa blueline and helped the team finish at the top of the Eastern Conference standings in 1998–99. By the 1999–2000 season most critics were touting him as a future Norris trophy winner.

### 1 SHAWN ANDERSON
5th Overall, 1986

The Buffalo Sabres had high hopes for this defenseman who excelled for the University of Maine and the Canadian National Team. During his first four NHL seasons, Anderson failed to earn a full-time place with the Sabres. Trades to Quebec, Washington, and Philadelphia did not improve his fortunes. He played his best hockey in the German Bundesliga and left the NHL in 1995 with 62 points in 255 games.

### 2 NEIL BRADY
3rd Overall, 1986

Brady was drafted by the New Jersey Devils after an excellent career as a playmaking centre with the Medicine Hat Tigers. He played only 29 NHL games in his first three pro seasons. In 1992–93, he was given a second chance by the expansion Ottawa Senators and scored their inaugural goal, but he was back in the minors before the end of the season.

### 3 DAVE CHYZOWSKI
2nd Overall, 1989

Heralded as a natural scorer with a devastating shot, Chyzowski scored 56 goals during his last season of junior with the Kamloops Blazers. He scored 14 points in 34 games as a rookie in 1989–90 with the New York Islanders and appeared in 56 games the following year. Over the next seven seasons he played all but 36 games in either the AHL or IHL.

### 4 DANIEL DORÉ
5th Overall, 1988

Doré was the second of two picks the Quebec Nordiques owned in the first five of the 1988 entry draft. During his four seasons in the QMJHL, Doré combined a rare blend of offensive talent with toughness. He played only 17 games for the Nords then spent the rest of his career in the minors.

## 5

### BRIAN LAWTON
1st Overall, 1983

Much fanfare followed the North Stars making Lawton the first
American chosen number one overall in the entry draft, though his
career was ultimately something of a disappointment. His pinnacle
came when he scored 21 goals 1986–87. Lawton played for six
NHL clubs and left the league in 1993 with 112 career goals.

## 6

### WAYNE McBEAN
4th Overall, 1987

While enjoying a stellar career with the powerful Medicine Hat
Tigers, superb offensive defenseman Wayne McBean was often
compared to Paul Coffey. As it turned out, he never played a full
NHL season and his best performance was the 19 points he scored
for the Islanders in 1990–91. McBean retired in 1994 with a mere 49
career points.

## 7

### JIM SANDLAK
4th Overall, 1985

A 6'4" right-winger who could score, Sandlak impressed all NHL
scouts and was the top ranked North American prospect during the
1984–85 mid-season ratings. Sandlak registered one 20-goal season
but did not rise above role player status for the Canucks.

## 8

### DOUG SMITH
2nd Overall, 1981

Smith was a top centre in the OHA with the Ottawa 67's. He played
decently for the L.A. Kings in parts of five seasons before a trade sent
him to Buffalo. For such a top prospect, a career-best 41 points was
a disappointment. Smith also skated for Edmonton, Vancouver, and
Pittsburgh before retiring with 115 career goals.

# Ten **SUCCESSFUL** NHLers **DRAFTED** by **LESSER-KNOWN** Teams

**1**

### BOB ESSENSA
Henry Carr Junior B, Toronto

Essensa was chosen by the Winnipeg Jets while he was still attending this well-known Toronto high school. He continued to play hockey at Michigan State before embarking on an NHL career that saw him win 130 games chiefly in Winnipeg.

Bob Essensa was drafted out of high school in Toronto and went on to a solid NHL caree

### BUTCH GORING
Dauphin Jr. A, Manitoba

Goring was a brilliant two-way centre who accumulated 888 points in sixteen NHL seasons. He recorded eight consecutive 20-goal seasons for the L.A. Kings before a trade sent him to the New York Islanders. Goring was a vital addition to a team that went on to win four consecutive Stanley Cups.

### PHIL HOUSLEY
South St. Paul High School, Minnesota

In 1982 the Buffalo Sabres chose Phil Housley sixth overall in the NHL Entry Draft. The smooth skater with a host of offensive gifts scored 66 points and was named to the NHL all-rookie team. He became one of the top offensive defensemen in the league and reached the 1,000-point mark in 1997–98.

### UWE KRUPP
Kolner EC, West Germany

The Buffalo Sabres took a shot at a 6' 6" defenseman playing in the West German league when they picked 223rd overall in the 1983 Entry Draft. Krupp played nearly five years on the Sabres' blueline then was sent to the Islanders as part of the Pierre Turgeon-Pat Lafontaine trade. He later scored the Cup-winning goal in overtime for the Colorado Avalanche in 1996.

### JOHN LeCLAIR
Bellows Free Academy, Vermont

The burly winger was a solid role player for the Montreal Canadiens and scored two key overtime goals when the team defeated Los Angeles to win the Stanley Cup in 1993. Following a trade to Philadelphia in 1995, he teamed with Eric Lindros and became one of the game's top power forwards with three straight 50-goal seasons.

## 6 REIJO RUOTSALAINEN
Karpat Oulu, Finland

Ruotsalainen was a gifted offensive defenseman who played parts of seven seasons in the NHL. The New York Rangers selected him 119th overall in 1980 and he went on to average 20 goals in the five seasons he spent there. He also helped the Edmonton Oilers win the Stanley Cup in 1987 and 1990 and was a star player in Switzerland.

## 7 GARY SARGENT
Fargo Moorheads, North Dakota

The Los Angeles Kings drafted this promising defenseman 48th over-all out of the Midwestern Junior Hockey League in 1974. He played three years with the Kings then joined Minnesota as a free agent in 1978. Sargent hit double figures in goals scored three times and played for the USA in the inaugural Canada Cup in 1976.

## 8 PETRI SKRIKO
SaiPa Lappeenranta, Finland

Originally chosen by Vancouver in 1981, Skriko reached the 30-goal mark four straight years from 1985–86 to 1988–89. He also played for Boston, Winnipeg, and San Jose before retiring in 1993 with 405 points in 541 career games.

## 9 JOZEF STUMPEL
AC Nitra, Czech Republic

Boston drafted Stumpel 40th overall in 1991. After a slow start he began to emerge as an impact player with 54- and 76-point seasons in 1996 and 1997. After being traded to Los Angeles, his career blossomed and in 1997–98 he had 79 points.

## 10 ERROL THOMPSON
Charlottetown Seniors, P.E.I.

The speedy Thompson was Toronto's second choice in 1970. He lat played with Darryl Sittler and Lanny McDonald on the club's top line and enjoyed a personal-high 43 goals in 1975–76. Thompson later played with Detroit and Pittsburgh and retired in 1981 with 2( career goals.

# First **TEN** American-Born **U.S. COLLEGE** or High School Players **DRAFTED** in the **FIRST** Round

**1**

### MIKE RAMSEY
Buffalo Sabres, 11th overall 1979

Somewhat lost in the hoopla surrounding the eligibility of many brilliant 18-year-olds was the selection of the steady Ramsey out of the University of Minnesota. He went on to play 1,070 regular season games, mostly with Buffalo. Ramsey scored 345 points, played exemplary defence, and was a respected team leader with the Sabres.

**2**

### BOBBY CARPENTER
Washington Capitals, 3rd overall 1981

The most anticipated American prospect up to that time, Carpenter was supposed to be chosen by the Hartford Whalers, based in his native New England. A trade between Colorado and Washington gave the latter a chance to draft ahead of the Whalers, much to the chagrin of the young phenom's family. He eventually settled in with the Caps and was a top scorer, including a 53-goal season in '84–'85.

**3**

### PHIL HOUSLEY
Buffalo Sabres, 6th overall 1982

star at South St. Paul High School in Minnesota, the swift-skating Housley made the transition to the NHL with ease. He scored 66 points in his first year and was selected to the NHL all-rookie team. Housley later played for Winnipeg, St. Louis, Calgary, New Jersey, and Washington and was placed on the NHL's second All-Star team in 1992. One of the top offensive rearguards of the 1980s, he reached the 1,000-point plateau during the 1997–98 season.

## 4

### BRIAN LAWTON
Minnesota North Stars, 1st overall 1983

Lawton was a highly-rated left-winger for the Mount St. Charles Academy high school team in his native New Jersey. The North Stars made him the first American to be taken with the first pick in the draft but in retrospect his NHL career did not justify this status. Lawton became a journeyman forward who skated with six teams. He recorded 112 career goals before retiring in 1993.

## 5

### TOM BARRASSO
Buffalo Sabres, 5th overall 1983

Barrasso became the first American goaltender drafted in the top five and quickly proved the Sabres right. In 1983–84 he won 26 games and was presented the Vézina and Calder trophies. Barrasso later joined Pittsburgh and backstopped the team to consecutive Stanley Cups in 1991 and 1992 before being traded to Ottawa late in the 1999–2000 schedule.

## 6

### DAVID JENSEN
Hartford Whalers, 20th overall 1983

Jensen was a first-rate goal scorer in high school with Lawrence Academy in Massachusetts . He enjoyed a solid year with the U.S. National team before debuting with Hartford in 1984–85. His NHL career never got untracked, however, and his best season was a 16-point year with the Washington Capitals in 1986–87.

## 7

### ED OLCZYK
Chicago Black Hawks, 3rd overall 1984

Olczyk was drafted by his hometown Blackhawks after excelling with the U.S. Olympic team at the Sarajevo games. He played hree years in Chicago before a blockbuster trade sent him to Toronto. He scored a career-high 42 goals for the Maple Leafs in 1987–88 and later played for Winnipeg, the New York Rangers, L.A., and Pittsburgh. Olczyk was part of the Rangers team that won the franchise's first Stanley Cup in 54 years in 1994.

### 8   AL IAFRATE
Toronto Maple Leafs, 4th overall 1984

An imposing combination of size and talent, Iafrate represented the U.S. at the 1984 Sarajevo Olympics before being chosen in the draft. In Toronto, he showed flashes of the brilliance expected of him with two, 20-goal seasons before a serious knee injury slowed him for nearly two years. Iafrate scored a personal-high 25 goals for Washington in 1992–93 and recorded the hardest shot in the league at the All-Star skills competition that same year.

### 9   DAVID QUINN
Minnesota North Stars, 13th overall 1983

Minnesota general manager Lou Nanne was thrilled to see Quinn still available when he chose in the 13th position. However, this proved to be a monumental disaster for the North Stars as the young Rhode Island native, who starred at Kent High School in Connecticut, never played above the level of Boston University, and was forced to retire early due to a life-threatening blood disorder.

### 10   TOM CHORSKE
Montreal Canadiens, 16th overall 1985

Chorske was an All-Star right-winger with the University of Minnesota before joining the Habs in 1989–90. He played sparingly with Montreal before he was sent to New Jersey in the deal involving Stephane Richer and Kirk Muller. Chorske gained a regular place in the Devils' line-up and helped the team win the Stanley Cup in 1995.

**1**    **BILLY BURCH**

Yonkers

Burch was a supreme forward who played most of his career with
the Hamilton Tigers/New York Americans franchise. In 1924–25 he
scored 20 goals in 24 games and was presented the Hart trophy. He
recorded a personal-high 22 goals the next year and the following
season won the Lady Byng trophy. Burch was elected to the
Hockey Hall of Fame in 1974 as a veteran player.

 **2**    **GUY HEBERT**

Troy

A talented netminder, Hebert played four years at Hamilton College,
in New York state and two seasons in the IHL before he got his first
taste of NHL action with St. Louis in 1991–92. His big break came
when the Mighty Ducks of Anaheim chose him in the 1993
Expansion Draft. Hebert won 20 games that first year and became
firmly entrenched as the club's starting goalie. In 1996–97 he
backstopped the Ducks to their first playoff appearance and a first-
round victory over the Phoenix Coyotes.

**3**    **ALEX LEVINSKY**

Syracuse

Levinsky was a solid defenseman who skated for three different clubs
in the 1930s. He was a member of the first Toronto Maple Leafs
Stanley Cup team in 1931–32 and took part in the historic Ace Bailey
benefit game in 1934. Levinsky played briefly for the New York
Rangers and then spent the last four-and-a-half years of his career in
Chicago. In 1938 he was a part of the Hawks' second championship
before retiring the next year after having played 367 games.

## 4 TODD MARCHANT
Buffalo

One of the NHL's speediest forwards, Marchant played an important role in the revitalization of the Edmonton Oilers in the late 1990s. His speed and tenacity made him one of the top checking forwards and penalty killers in the league. Marchant also chipped in with a few goals, none bigger than the game seven overtime winner when his club upset the Dallas Stars in the 1997 Western Conference quarter-final.

## 5 BRIAN MULLEN
New York City

The younger brother of Joey Mullen, Brian was a consistent scorer from the right-wing throughout his eleven-year NHL tenure. He recorded six 20-goal seasons along with a career best 32 in 1984–85. Mullen represented the U.S. at 1984 Canada Cup and the World Championships in 1989 and 1991. Sadly, his career was ended by a heart attack suffered during training camp in 1993. In 1995 Mullen was presented the Lester Patrick Award in honour of his service to hockey in the U.S.

Brian Mullen came from the inner city of New York
to represent both the NHL and USA Hockey
with great integrity.

### 6 JOEY MULLEN
New York City

The soft-spoken Mullen was one of the most productive American forwards in NHL history. He was originally signed as a free agent by the St. Louis Blues for whom he recorded consecutive 40-goal seasons in 1983–84 and 1984–85. An unpopular trade saw him shipped to Calgary where he won a Stanley Cup in 1989. Mullen later helped Pittsburgh win consecutive Stanley Cups in 1991 and 1992. On February 7, 1995, he became the first American to reach 1,000 career points and a little over two years later he became the first from his country to score 500 goals.

### 7 MATHIEU SCHNEIDER
New York City

A talented offensive defenseman, Schneider was drafted by Montreal out of the respected Cornwall Royals' program of the OHL. He was a part of a Stanley Cup championship in 1993 and registered a career-high 20 goals the next year. He later played with the Islanders and Maple Leafs and helped the U.S. win the inaugural World Cup of hockey in 1996.

# Eight Players from **CLEVELAND** to **PLAY** for **MINNESOTA** after the **MERGER** of **1979**

**1**

### JOHN BABY

This unfortunate surname is an apt metaphor for a brief career in the NHL. Baby played just 24 games with Cleveland, but although he was taken by Minnesota, he was put in the lineup for only two games for the Stars that year and in short order was out of the NHL for good.

**2**

### DANIEL CHICOINE

Chicoine did not exactly set the Stars on fire after being placed on the Reserve List from the Dispersal Draft. He had played just six games for the Barons in '77–'78 and wound up in just one game for the North Stars the next year and 24 the following season.

**3**

### MIKE FIDLER

A 124-game veteran of the Barons, Fidler played parts of the next three seasons in Minnesota before his career slowly fizzled into the minors. In seven NHL seasons, he never was involved in even one playoff game.

**4**

### AL MacADAM

One of the few stars of the Barons, MacAdam developed into a 40-goal scorer for the North Stars and was a key man in the team's drive to the '81 Cup finals. His goal production dipped after that, and he was traded to the Vancouver Canucks prior to the '84–'85 season.

**5**

### KRIS MANERY

A prospect Minnesota wanted to take a chance on, Manery's stock dropped quickly after moving into the North Stars' lineup. He played 60 games his first year, but just 28 the year after before being traded to Vancouver. Once there, he lasted only 21 games before being sent to the Jets in Winnipeg, his third team of the season and his last full year in the league.

### 6 DENNIS MARUK

The pick of the litter by far, Maruk improved once he was out of Cleveland. He played just two games with Minnesota in '78–'79 before being traded to Washington, but with the Caps he scored 30 goals that year and after a middling '79–'80 followed with seasons of 50 and 60 goals.

### 7 GILLES MELOCHE

One of the great targets of the 1970s, Meloche played nine seasons before seeing the playoffs and rarely played on a winning team. His lifetime 3.64 goals against attests to the quality of those teams, as his 788 games confirms his status as a bona fide goalie. After being claimed by Minnesota, he stayed seven years with the team, the last six qualifying for the postseason.

### 8 GREG SMITH

Smith had a fruitful 829-game NHL career with five teams, three of those years coming with the North Stars after the Dispersal Draft. A defensive defenseman, he scored just 56 career goals. He was usually a minus player in the +/– standings and, not surprisingly, rarely played on a .500 team.

# **SEVEN** Most Important
# **GAMES** Played in **CALIFORNIA**

**1**

**FEBRUARY 27, 1960**

Squaw Valley,    United States 3  USSR 2

The highly-talented Soviets were stymied by U.S. goalie Jack McCartan during the most critical game of the Squaw Valley Olympics. The Americans finished their gold medal performance with a 9–4 rout of Czechoslovakia the next day.

**2**

**OCTOBER 18, 1967**

First NHL game between inter-state rivals

The initial encounter between these two rivals from the Golden State took place at the Oakland Alameda Coliseum. The Kings took a 2–1 lead in the third period but the home side equalized on a goal by veteran defenseman Kent Douglas.

**3**

**FEBRUARY 10, 1981**

33rd NHL All-Star Game, at L.A. Forum

The host Campbell Conference defeated their Wales counterparts by a 4–1 score. The home crowd went wild as the "Triple Crown Line" of Marcel Dionne, Charlie Simmer, and Dave Taylor was left ntact and goalie Mario Lessard played the last half of the game.

**4**

**APRIL 15, 1989**

Great Western Forum  L.A. 6  Edmonton 3

In the most emotional moment during Wayne Gretzky's first year with the Los Angeles Kings, he scored an empty net goal to eliminate his former team from the playoffs. Los Angeles went on to win the game 6–3 and the series four games to three.

**5**

**JUNE 5, 1993**

Great Western Forum   Montreal 4   Los Angeles 3 (OT)

he first Stanley Cup final game played in California was a thriller. he visitors took a 3–0 only to see L.A. even things up courtesy of goal by Wayne Gretzky late in the third period. John LeClair poiled the party by scoring at just 34 seconds into overtime.

## 6 MAY 10, 1994
San Jose Arena    San Jose 5    Toronto 2

Sparked by Sergei Makarov's breakaway goal in the first period, the Sharks took a 3–2 lead over the Maple Leafs to come within one game of the Stanley Cup semi-finals. The Sharks lost the last two games at Maple Leaf Gardens but earned league-wide respect in their third NHL season.

## 7 JANUARY 23, 1995
Paul Kariya's first home game with the Mighty Ducks of Anaheim

Fans at the Arrowhead Pond of Anaheim were treated to their first glimpse of superstar Paul Kariya. The Ducks defeated Edmonton 5–4 in overtime during a spirited home opener. Kariya went on to score 50 goals the next year and later formed one of the NHL's most dangerous forward combinations with Teemu Selanne.

Sergei Makarov helped San Jose to respectability in the early stages of the franchise's entry into the NHL.

# FIRST NHL GAMES Played by the 1967-75 EXPANSION Teams

**1**

### BUFFALO SABRES    OCTOBER 10, 1970

Buffalo Sabres 2    Pittsburgh Penguins 1

The Buffalo Sabres began their first NHL season with a 2–1 victory in Pittsburgh courtesy of Gilbert Perreault's winning goal. Perreault then went on to win the Calder Trophy and the team notched a respectable 63 points.

**2**

### LOS ANGELES KINGS OCTOBER 14, 1967

Los Angeles Kings 4    Philadelphia Flyers 2

After spotting the visiting Flyers a 2–0 lead, the Kings roared back to win at the Long Beach Arena. Brian Kilrea scored twice for L.A. The team finished second in the West Division standings then were defeated by Minnesota in a tough quarterfinal series.

**3**

### NEW YORK ISLANDERS  OCTOBER 7, 1972

Atlanta Flames 3    New York Islanders 2

The NHL's two newest teams hooked up for the season opener at the Nassau Coliseum. Rey Comeau scored the winner for Atlanta and Ed Westfall notched the first goal for the Islanders who eventually became one of the NHL's elite teams.

**4**

### PHILADELPHIA FLYERS  OCTOBER 11, 1967

Oakland Seals 5    Philadelphia Flyers 1

Although they eventually became the first expansion team to win the Cup, the Flyers absorbed a sound beating their first NHL game. Bill Sutherland's first goal in franchise history was the only point of note in this contest.

**5**

### PITTSBURGH PENGUINS OCTOBER 11, 1967

Montreal Canadiens 2    Pittsburgh Penguins 1

The Penguins began their NHL sojourn against one of hockey's most famous teams. Two legends of the game figured prominently in this contest. Andy Bathgate scored Pittsburgh's first NHL goal while Jean Béliveau notched the winner for the Habs.

## 6 ST. LOUIS BLUES  OCTOBER 11, 1967
St. Louis Blues 2    Minnesota North Stars 2

The St. Louis Blues opened their inaugural NHL season with a 2–2 tie against expansion cousins the Minnesota North Stars. Larry Keenan scored the first Blues goal. Wayne Rivers was credited with tying the game.

## 7 VANCOUVER CANUCKS  OCTOBER 9, 1970
Los Angeles Kings 3    Vancouver Canucks 2

The Vancouver Canucks were the first Canadian team apart from the Canadiens and Maple Leafs since the Montreal Maroons folded in 1938. They began by dropping a 3–2 decision at home to the Los Angeles Kings. Defenseman Barry Wilkins scored the first goal for the Canucks. Bob Berry scored twice for the winners.

## 8 WASHINGTON CAPITALS  OCTOBER 9, 1974
New York Rangers 6    Washington Capitals 3

The Washington Capitals initiated a dreadful first season by losing 6–3 at home to the New York Rangers. Jim Hrycuik scored the team' first NHL goal. The Capitals only managed 21 points that year and missed the playoffs in each of their first eight seasons.

# Eight **GREATEST MOMENTS**
## from the **"IGLOO"**

### MARCH 24, 1976
Jean Pronovost's 50th goal

During a 5–5 tie with the Boston Bruins, Jean Pronovost became the first member of the Penguins and 14th player in NHL history to record a 50-goal season. The classy winger beat Gilles Gilbert to reach his milestone.

### APRIL 26, 1976
New York Islanders complete playoff comeback

The New York Islanders completed the most stirring playoff comeback since the 1942 Maple Leafs by beating Pittsburgh 1–0 in the seventh game of the quarter-finals. The Penguins had led the series 3–0 but the Long Islanders didn't give up and eventually won courtesy of a shutout by Glenn "Chico" Resch.

"Chico" Resch was one of the more colourful goalies during his career in the NHL.

**3**

Game MVP Mario Lemieux delighted the home audience by leading the Wales Conference to a 12–7 win over their Campbell foes. The "Magnificent One" became only the second player after Wayne Gretzky to score four goals in an All-Star Game.

**4**

MAY 15, 1991

Game 1 Stanley Cup final

Expansion cousins Pittsburgh and Minnesota met in the first Stanley Cup final game ever played at the Civic Arena. The North Stars won the opener 5–4 but the Mario Lemieux-led Penguins ultimately claimed the Cup in six games.

**5**

FEBRUARY 7, 1995

Joe Mullen's 1,000th point

While helping the Penguins clobber the Florida Panthers 7–3, Joe Mullen became the first American to record 1,000 NHL points. Two years later he became the first to score 500 goals during a Pens-Colorado game in Denver.

**6**

JUNE 1, 1996

Florida Panthers reach the Stanley Cup final

In only their third year of existence, the upstart Florida Panthers stunned the Civic Arena crowd by defeating the home town Penguins 3–1 in the seventh game of the Eastern Conference final. The underdogs utilized team speed, smothering defense, and opportunistic scoring to eliminate the Pens.

## 7

Mario Lemieux's last home game

After helping to keep the Pens alive in the Eastern Conference quarter-finals against Philadelphia, Lemieux circled the ice to pay tribute to his home town fans. This turned out to be his last game at the "Igloo" as Pittsburgh lost in Philly to bow out of the series in five games.

## 8

FEBRUARY 15, 1999

First game as the NHL's oldest arena

Two days after the last game played at Maple Leaf Gardens, the Penguins hosted the Washington Capitals. The home side won 7–3 in the first match played in the "Igloo" when it had become the NHL's oldest arena.

# Four **PLAYERS** Who **SKATED**
# for the **MOST EXPANSION** Teams

**1**

## JEAN-JACQUES DAIGNEAULT — 9

(Vancouver, Philadelphia, St. Louis,
Pittsburgh, Anaheim, N.Y. Islanders, Nashville,
Phoenix, Minnesota)

An offensive defenseman, Daigneault debuted with the Vancouver
Canucks in 1984–85. He later helped Philadelphia reach the finals
in 1987 and was part of the Habs' Stanley Cup win in 1992–93.
Other than Montreal, he played strictly for expansion teams.

**2**

## MICHEL PETIT — 8

(Vancouver, Quebec, Calgary, Los Angeles,
Tampa Bay, Edmonton, Philadelphia, Phoenix)

A rugged defenseman with decent offensive skills, Petit was
Vancouver's first-round draft choice in 1982. Some 800 regular
season games later, he had scored in excess of 300 points on eight
expansion teams plus two Original Six franchises.

**3**

## DAN QUINN — 8

(Calgary, Pittsburgh, Vancouver, St. Louis,
Philadelphia, Minnesota, Ottawa, Los Angeles)

A clever offensive forward who amassed nearly 700 career points,
Quinn helped the Flames reach the finals in 1986. He was also the
only player to skate for all six 1967 expansion teams because
Minnesota was a hybrid of their original franchise plus the
Oakland/California Seals.

**4**

## BILL HOULDER — 7

(Washington, Buffalo, Anaheim, St. Louis,
Tampa Bay, San Jose, Nashville)

A true journeyman, Houlder was a playmaking defenseman in junior
who became a solid positional rearguard in the NHL. Along the way
he debuted with the Washington Capitals and was a member of
Anaheim's inaugural team in 1993–94.

# Eight Best **GOALTENDING**
# **TANDEMS** Since Expansion

**1**

### GUMP WORSLEY AND ROGIE VACHON
Montreal Canadiens (1967–69)

The veteran Worsley and the youngster Vachon formed an effective goaltending partnership. After the 1967–68 season, they shared the Vézina Trophy and helped the Habs win consecutive Stanley Cups in 1968 and 1969. In addition, Worsley was the placed on the NHL first All-Star Team in 1968.

**2**

### GLENN HALL AND JACQUES PLANTE
St. Louis Blues (1968–70)

Fans of the expansion Blues were treated to great goalkeeping by veterans Plante and Hall in the late 1960s. In 1968–69 the two captured the Vézina trophy and helped the Blues win the West Division playoff championship and a birth in the Stanley Cup final.

**3**

### ED GIACOMIN AND GILLES VILLEMURE
New York Rangers (1970–75)

This outstanding duo contributed significantly to the Rangers becoming one of the elite teams in the NHL during the early 1970s. They shared the Vézina trophy in 1971 and helped New York register three straight 100-point seasons and reach the 1972 Stanley Cup finals.

**4**

### DON EDWARDS AND BOB SAUVE
Buffalo Sabres (1977–81)

The Sabres were one of the NHL's strongest defensive clubs in the late 1970s. Both Edwards and Sauve enjoyed their best seasons playing in western New York and shared the Vézina trophy in 1980. Their stellar play helped the team reach the semi-finals in 1980 for the first time since 1975.

**5**

## BILLY SMITH AND ROLAND MELANSON
New York Islanders (1980–84)

When the Islanders dominated the NHL in the early 1980s, Smith was the undisputed first string goalie on the team. In 1981–82 Melanson emerged as a quality netminder and played 117 regular season games in three seasons which helped keep Smith fresh for the playoffs. In 1982, Smith won the Vézina trophy, and the following year Melanson finished as the runner-up to Pete Peeters of Boston. The tandem won the William M. Jennings trophy in 1983 and helped the Isles win their fourth straight Stanley Cup.

**6**

## PAT RIGGIN AND AL JENSEN
Washington Capitals (1982–85)

A large part of the Caps' ascendance to respectability in the 1980s was the consistent play of their two netminders. In 1983–84, Riggin led the NHL in shutouts and goals against average and the pair won the Jennings trophy for allowing the fewest goals in the league.

**7**

## PATRICK ROY AND BRIAN HAYWARD
Montreal Canadiens (1986–1990)

Roy was one of the top goalies of his era and won consecutive Vézina trophies in 1988–89 and 1989–90. He was ably teamed with Hayward who won 20 games in both 1987–88 and 1988–89. The two combined to win three consecutive Jennings trophies beginning in 1987 and helped Montreal reach the Stanley Cup final in 1989.

**8**

## ANDY MOOG AND RÉJEAN LEMELIN
Boston Bruins (1988–93)

When the Bruins acquired Moog late in the 1987–88 season, their goaltending became one of the strongest in the NHL. The two won the Jennings trophy in 1990 and helped the Bruins reach the Stanley Cup final in 1988 and 1990. Boston also topped the 100-point mark three times with this excellent tandem in net.

# Ten **UNDER-RATED DEFENSEMEN**
## from the **1970s**

**1**

### DON AWREY

Awrey was a solid defensive blueliner during his 17 NHL seasons. Many considered him the toughest player in one-on-one situations. He was an important member of two Boston Bruins Stanley Cup wins and represented Canada in the historic Summit Series versus the USSR in 1972.

**2**

### GARY BERGMAN

A fine skater and superb passer, Bergman played the majority of his 838 career games with the Detroit Red Wings. He accumulated 367 career points and was an integral part of the victorious Canadian team in the 1972 Summit Series against the USSR.

**3**

### DAVE BURROWS

An excellent defensive player, Burrows was one of the fastest backwards skaters in the NHL. During his decade of service in the NHL, the steady rearguard recorded 164 points and took part in three NHL All-Star Games.

**4**

### BILL HAJT

One of the league's more relentless checkers in his own zone, Hajt frustrated opposing forwards during the 1970s. He was an important reason why the Sabres made the Stanley Cup final in 1975 and consistently recorded one of the league's lowest goals against averages.

**5**

### DENNIS KEARNS

A nifty playmaker, Kearns played every one of his 677 NHL games with the Vancouver Canucks. He registered 321 career points and set a team record for defensemen with 60 points in 1977.

Bill Hajt helped anchor the Buffalo defence during the team's ascendance in the 197[

**6**

## DAVE MALONEY

A fine offensive defenseman and respected team leader, Maloney played 657 games, mostly with the New York Rangers. He reached double figures in goals scored four times and captained the "Blueshirts" to an appearance in the 1979 Stanley Cup final.

**7**

## DICK REDMOND

Redmond was one of the more reliable offensive defense-men in the 1970s. He divided his 771 career games between six teams and registered 445 points. In 1973 Redmond scored six points in the playoffs during the Chicago Blackhawks' drive to the Stanley Cup final.

**8**

## ROD SEILING

Seiling was a solid player in his own end who also head-manned the puck effectively during his 979 NHL games. He recorded 331 career points, helped the Rangers reach the Stanley Cup final once, and played with Team Canada during the 1972 Summit Series against the Soviet Union.

**9**

## DALLAS SMITH

On a team blessed with Bobby Orr, Dallas Smith's consistent play was often forgotten. He scored 307 career points in nearly 900 games and helped Boston win the Stanley Cup in 1970 and 1972. He was also the NHL's plus/minus leader in 1967–68 while taking a regular shift on the Bruins' blueline.

**10**

## RON STACKHOUSE

Stackhouse was an excellent offensive defenseman in a career spent chiefly with the Pittsburgh Penguins. He hit double figures in goals scored twice, registered 459 career points, and was selected to play in the 1980 NHL All-Star Game.

# Ten Best **DEFENSEMEN** to Play for the Chicago **BLACKHAWKS**

**1**

### TAFFY ABEL

Abel was one of hockey's most reliable defensive bluelin-ers in the 1920s and 1930s. He spent five years with the Blackhawks after three solid years as Ching Johnson's partner in New York. During his last NHL season he anchored the Chicago blueline when the team won its first Stanley Cup in 1934.

**2**

### CHRIS CHELIOS

A tough competitor with exemplary offensive and defensive skills, Chelios was acquired by the Hawks from Montreal for Denis Savard prior to the 1990–91 season. He became the anchor on the team's blueline and won the Norris trophy in 1993 and 1996. In 1992, Chelios was a key factor in the team's drive to the Stanley Cup finals.

**3**

### BILL GADSBY

A talented playmaker with tremendous poise, Gadsby played his first eight years in Chicago. He later excelled with New York and Detroit before retiring in 1966 with 568 points in 1,248 games. The charismatic veteran was elected to the Hockey Hall of Fame in 1970.

**4**

### PIERRE PILOTE

A reliable defenseman with fine playmaking skills, Pilote won three straight Norris trophies from 1963 to 1965. He was a member of the Hawks' 1961 Stanley Cup team and was a five-time selection to the NHL first All-Star Team. He retired in 1969 with 498 career points and was elected to the Hockey Hall of Fame in 1975.

## 5 EARL SEIBERT

One of the NHL's brightest stars of the 1930s and 1940s, Seibert played most of his fifteen NHL seasons in the Windy City. He played on the team's 1938 Stanley Cup championship and was a four-time selection to the NHL first All-Star Team. He retired in 1946 with 276 career points and was elected to the Hockey Hall of Fame in 1963.

## 6 PAT STAPLETON

A skilled playmaker from his blueline position, Stapleton spent eight seasons in Chicago. He formed one of the top blueline tandems in the NHL with Bill White and was voted to the NHL second All-Star Team three times. "Whitey" left the NHL in 1973 with 337 points in 635 matches.

## 7 ELMER VASKO

"Moose" Vasko was one of the more imposing NHL defensemen of his era. Between 1957 and 1966 he played a key role on the Hawks' blueline and helped the team win the Stanley Cup in 1961. Vasko was selected to the NHL second All-Star Team in 1962–63 and 1963–64 before retiring in 1966. He returned the next year to play three seasons in Minnesota before ending his career permanently in 1970.

## 8 BILL WHITE

One of the best positional defensemen of his era, White spent most of his ten years in the league with the Blackhawks. He formed one of the top defensive pairings in the NHL with Pat Stapleton and helped the club reach the Stanley Cup finals in 1971 and 1973. White's steady play was recognized by his three consecutive selections to the NHL second All-Star Team from 1972 to 1974.

### 9 DOUG WILSON

Wilson spent 14 of his 16 NHL seasons with the Blackhawks. A solid positional player, he possessed one of the hardest shots in the NHL. In 1981–82 Wilson registered a career-high 39 goals and won the Norris trophy. He was placed on the NHL second All-Star Team twice and retired with career totals of 237 goals, 827 points.

### 10 STEVE SMITH

A member of the Hawks' blueline corps from 1991–92 to 1996–97, Smith was a punishing hitter with a feared shot from the point. He helped the team reach the Stanley Cup finals in 1992 and teamed with Chris Chelios on one of the top defensive tandems in the NHL.

### 1 IVAN BOLDIREV

A talented stick-handler and scorer, Boldirev was acquired from Boston in November 1971. He scored 52 goals in three seasons for the Seals while showing flashes of his immense potential that was later realized in Chicago.

### 2 BILL HICKE

A fine all-round right-winger, Hicke became one of California's first offensive heroes. In 1967–68 and 1968–69 he registered consecutive 20-goal seasons and scored 61 goals overall for the Seals in 188 games.

### 3 JOEY JOHNSON

Johnson was a legitimate scorer who would have produced more on a better team. As it was, he had 84 goals for California, including a career best 28 in 1972–73.

### 4 REGGIE LEACH

Leach gave fans a peak into the future when he registered consecutive 20-goal seasons for the Seals in 1973 and 1974. He was eventually sent to the Flyers in the deal that brought Al MacAdam to the West Coast.

### 5 DENNIS MARUK

The greatest scorer in franchise history, Maruk was drafted 1st overall by the Seals in 1975. He scored 30 goals as a rookie in 1975–76 and developed into a top-level scoring star when the club relocated to Cleveland.

## 6 GILLES MELOCHE

After being acquired from Chicago, Meloche burst on the scene with four shutouts for the Seals in 1971–72. The next year he led all NHL goalies in minutes played and ended up spending five seasons with California. Meloche remained with the club when it was shifted to Cleveland and later merged with Minnesota.

## 7 DOUG ROBERTS

Roberts was a workhorse on the Seals' blueline for three years beginning in 1968–69. He appeared in all but four games and was often the club's steadiest influence in their own zone.

## 8 GARY SIMMONS

The "Snake" enjoyed two fine seasons with the Seals when he generally kept his club in the game. He won 25 games over the 1974–75 and 1975–76 seasons and recorded four shutouts, impressive numbers considering he played on a relatively weak team.

## 9 GARY SMITH

Smith joined the Seals during their inaugural season in 1967–68. During the next four years he was peppered with rubber but managed 21 wins in 1968–69 and a league-high 71 appearances in 1970–71.

## 10 CAROL VADNAIS

A fine offensive performer at forward and as point man on the power-play, Vadnais scored 63 goals in parts of four seasons with the Seals. He was the club's representative in three NHL All-Star Gamess.

Few remember Reggie Leach's brief time with Oakland before he arrived in Philadelphia.

### **DAVE KEON**
Noranda

One of the finest two-way centres in the history of the game, Keon scored 20 goals as a rookie in 1960–61 and won the Calder Trophy. He was an integral part of Toronto's four Stanley Cup triumphs in the 1960s and was the Conn Smythe Trophy winner in 1967. The smooth-skating star was elected to the Hockey Hall of Fame in 1986.

### **LORNE CHABOT**
Montreal

"Sad Eyes" Chabot was one of the top goalies in the 1930s. He recorded seven, 20-win seasons and helped Toronto win its first Stanley Cup as the Maple Leafs, in 1932. Chabot recorded 33 shutouts in five years with Toronto.

### **VINCENT DAMPHOUSSE**
Montreal

A fine offensive centre and left-winger, Damphousse was Toronto's top draft choice in 1986. In 1989–90, he played left wing with Tom Fergus and Daniel Marois. He promptly scored 94 points and broke Frank Mahovlich's single season record.

### **MARCEL PRONOVOST**
Shawinigan Falls

Although he played most of his career in Detroit, Pronovost added valuable experience to the Toronto blueline from 1965 to 1970. He played 223 games for the Maple Leafs and was a member of the 196 Stanley Cup team.

### **FELIX POTVIN**
Anjou

During his first two NHL seasons, Potvin led the Maple Leafs to consecutive appearances in the Stanley Cup semi-finals. He won more than 150 games in eight seasons with Toronto while registering 12 shutouts.

**TOD SLOAN**
Pontiac

An excellent all-round forward, Sloan played nearly a decade with the Maple Leafs including the 1951 championship season. Twice he topped the 30-goal mark and he was placed on the NHL second All-Star Team in 1956.

 **IAN TURNBULL**
Montreal

One of the most naturally talented offensive defensemen of the 1970s, Turnbull formed an excellent partnership with Borje Salming for several years. In 1977 he set an NHL record for rearguards by scoring five goals in game.

 **JIM MORRISON**
Montreal

A solid positional defenseman, Morrsion spent parts of seven years in Toronto in the 1950s. Between 1955 and 1957 he was a member of the NHL team that faced the Stanley Cup champions in the All-Star Game.

 **SYLVAIN LEFEBVRE**
Richmond

Although he was only in Toronto for two seasons, Lefebvre was a key defender on one of the NHL's stingiest clubs. His excellent work helped the Maple Leafs reach the semi-finals in both 1993 and 1994.

 **JACQUES PLANTE**
Shawinigan Falls

Plante played nearly three full seasons with Toronto in the early 1970s while solidifying its goaltending position. In 1970–71 he led the NHL with a 1.88 goals against mark and was placed on the NHL second All-Star Team.

# Seven **KEY TRADES** between **TORONTO** and **MONTREAL**

**1**

## OCTOBER 1, 1933

George Hainsworth to Toronto for Lorne Chabot

Hainsworth led the NHL in wins his first two years in Toronto and recorded 20 shutouts. Chabot registered eight shutouts with Montreal but was soon traded in the deal that sent Lionel Conacher to the Canadiens.

**2**

## MARCH 6, 1943

Ted Kennedy to Toronto for Frank Eddolls

Kennedy led the Maple Leafs to five Stanley Cups and was elected to the Hockey Hall of Fame in 1966. Eddolls played just 57 games for Montreal before joining the New York Rangers.

**3**

## JUNE 26, 1975

Doug Jarvis to Montreal for Greg Hubick

Jarvis was a key defensive centre on four Stanley Cup teams in Montreal and later set the NHL's Iron Man record by appearing in 964 straight games. Hubick scored only 14 points in one season with the Maple Leafs.

**4**

## MARCH 10, 1981

Michel Larocque to Toronto for Robert Picard

Larocque fought bravely for 74 games in the Toronto goal while rarely seeing any defensive support. Picard played parts of three seasons in Montreal before he was traded to Winnipeg for the 3rd-round draft pick that the Habs used to draft Patrick Roy.

**5**

## DECEMBER 17, 1982

Dan Daoust to Toronto for a 3rd-round draft choice (later sent to Minnesota)

Dan Daoust was an offensive sparkplug during his first three years in Toronto before switching to the role of checking centre. He played 518 games with the Maple Leafs while the Habs took comfort in the fact that they decided to keep Guy Carbonneau ahead of Daoust.

## 6

### NOVEMBER 7, 1988
Russ Courtnall to Montreal for John Kordic and a 6th-round draft choice (Michael Doers)

Courtnall hit the 20-goal mark three straight years for the Habs. Kordic was a role player with Toronto in parts of three seasons while Doers never played in the NHL.

## 7

### AUGUST 20, 1992
Sylvain Lefebvre to Toronto for a 3rd-round draft choice (Martin Belanger)

Lefebvre developed into one of the best defensive defensemen in the NHL while helping the Maple Leafs reach consecutive semi-finals in 1993 and 1994. Belanger never made an impact with the Habs.

### 1

**PETER MAHOVLICH**

117 points 1974–75

Mahovlich centred the Habs' top line with Guy Lafleur and Steve Shutt and recorded a remarkable 82 assists. "The Little M" was agile for a big man and was able to use his 6'5" size to advantage when necessary. His play helped the Habs finish with 113 points and reach the Stanley Cup semi-finals that season.

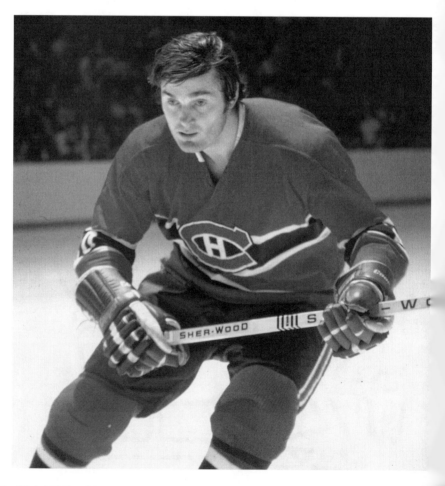

The "Little M," Pete Mahovlich, was a consistent and outstanding scorer with Montreal in the 197▮

### PETER MAHOVLICH
105 points 1975-76

Mahovlich enjoyed a second straight year of scoring 100 points and was among the league leaders with 71 assists. His strong play was a key factor in Montreal's 127-point regular season and Stanley Cup championship. In all, Mahovlich played on four Stanley Cup winners in Montreal.

### JACQUES LEMAIRE
97 points 1977-78

Lemaire replaced the traded Pete Mahovlich on the Habs' top line with Lafleur and Shutt. Like his predecessor, he was among the league leaders with 61 assists while excelling on both speciality teams. That year Lemaire was a key component of the club's second straight Stanley Cup triumph.

### VINCENT DAMPHOUSSE
97 points 1992-93

The Habs coveted Damphousse during his first six NHL seasons and jumped at the chance to acquire him prior to the 1992–93 season. He responded with a career-high 97 points while helping the team win the Stanley Cup.

### PIERRE TURGEON
96 points 1995-96

"Lucky Pierre" thrived as captain of the Habs the year they moved from the Forum to the Molson Centre. After a slow start, the team played well the rest of the season and lost a tough six game series to the New York Rangers in the Eastern Conference quarter-finals.

### JACQUES LEMAIRE
95 points 1972-73

Blessed with speed and a hard shot, Lemaire broke through with 44 goals while playing on a line with Yvan Cournoyer and Chuck Lefley. Later that year he scored 20 points in 17 playoff games as the Habs defeated Chicago in the Stanley Cup finals.

### KIRK MULLER
94 points 1992-93

A feisty leader with a an ability to score, Muller enjoyed his finest NHL in his first year with Montreal. The next season he contributed ten goals and 17 points in the Habs' drive to a Stanley Cup championship.

### VINCENT DAMPHOUSSE
94 points 1995-96

Damphousse was an experienced offensive threat on a young and improving Habs team that rebounded from an 0-5 start. He was arguably the club's top player with eight points in the opening round playoff loss to the New York Rangers.

### BOBBY SMITH
93 points 1987-88

A former scoring star with the Minnesota North Stars, Smith helped the Habs win the Stanley Cup in 1986 and enjoyed his best season two years later. He retired in 1993 with 357 goals and 1,036 points to his credit.

### JACQUES LEMAIRE
92 points 1974-75

Lemaire scored 36 goals and 56 assists while combining with Pete Mahovlich to give Montreal the most depth in the league at centre. He was a key performer on the Habs' power-play and penalty killing units and helped the team register 113 points and reach the Stanley Cup semi-finals.

## ACKNOWLEDGEMENTS

Andrew Podnieks would like to thank the various emotional contributors to the making of the book. To Jack David, Jen Hale, Wiesia Kolasinska, Mary Bowness, Tracey Millen, and Amy Logan at ECW for their time and patience. To Tania Craan, for perfection in design excellence. To Peter Jaggles for resisting the temptation to resort to litigation to become part of this project. To those at the Hockey Hall of Fame who are forever and happily custodians of the game's history, namely Phil Pritchard, Craig Campbell, Darren Boyko, Tyler Wolosowich (the scan man), Izak Westgate, Geoff Fletcher, Jacqueline Boughazale, Marilyn Robbins, Margaret Lockhart, and Dave Sandford. To Jon Redfern, Billy Yamamoto, and Geri Dasgupta. To Liz, Ian, Zack, Emily, and my mom for a treat down East to keep me sane.

Jeff Davis would like to thank the following providers of moral and practical support. To Peggy for all her love and patience and our children Ian and Julia for keeping me in "game shape." To my parents, grandparents, and friends who offered plenty of encouragement and interest. To the stellar line-up at the Hockey Hall of Fame for a wealth of information and for sharing their passion for the game. To Jack David, Jen Hale, Wiesia Kolasinska, Tania Craan, Mary Bowness, Tracey Millen, and Amy Logan at ECW for a consistently high standard of work and for allowing my kids to disrupt their office. To anybody reading this book who is inspired to start an argument.